CONFERENCE PROCEEDINGS

For Whom the Whistle Blows

Advancing Corporate Compliance and Integrity Efforts in the Era of Dodd-Frank

Michael D. Greenberg

 RAND Center for Corporate Ethics and Governance

A RAND INSTITUTE FOR CIVIL JUSTICE CENTER

This report was funded with pooled resources from the RAND Center for Corporate Ethics and Governance, which is part of the RAND Institute for Civil Justice, a unit of the RAND Corporation.

Library of Congress Cataloging-in-Publication Data

For whom the whistle blows : advancing corporate compliance and integrity efforts in the era of Dodd-Frank / Michael D. Greenberg.
    p. cm.
  Includes bibliographical references.
  ISBN 978-0-8330-5893-5 (pbk. : alk. paper)
  1. Corporate governance—Law and legislation—United States—Congresses. 2. Whistle blowing—Law and legislation—United States—Congresses. 3. Financial services industry—Law and legislation—United States—Congresses. 4. United States. Dodd-Frank Wall Street Reform and Consumer Protection Act—Congresses. 5. Securities fraud—United States—Congresses. I. Greenberg, Michael D., 1969-

  KF1422.A75F67 2011
  345.73'0268—dc23

                                                                              2011037238

The RAND Corporation is a nonprofit institution that helps improve policy and decisionmaking through research and analysis. RAND's publications do not necessarily reflect the opinions of its research clients and sponsors.

RAND® is a registered trademark.

Cover image courtesy of iStockphoto/keithfrith. Used with permission.

Published 2011 by the RAND Corporation
1776 Main Street, P.O. Box 2138, Santa Monica, CA 90407-2138
1200 South Hayes Street, Arlington, VA 22202-5050
4570 Fifth Avenue, Suite 600, Pittsburgh, PA 15213-2665
RAND URL: http://www.rand.org/
To order RAND documents or to obtain additional information, contact
Distribution Services: Telephone: (310) 451-7002;
Fax: (310) 451-6915; Email: order@rand.org

PREFACE

The 2010 passage of new federal whistleblower provisions under the Dodd-Frank Wall Street Reform and Consumer Protection Act invited significant controversy, and critics and advocates have squared off regarding the likely impact of the new rules on corporations and their employees. On May 11, 2011, the RAND Corporation convened a symposium in Washington, D.C., that focused on the challenges to the private sector posed by the whistleblower provisions under Dodd-Frank and on the opportunities to reinforce internal compliance programs within the new legal environment. Invited participants at the symposium included thought leaders from the ranks of public company directors and executives, ethics and compliance officers, and stakeholders from the government, industry, academic, and nonprofit sectors. Discussions focused on the probable impact of the new whistleblower rules on corporate America; on the importance of internal compliance and reporting efforts to corporations, regulators, and employees alike; and on concrete steps that could be taken to make compliance and internal reporting mechanisms stronger in the era of Dodd-Frank.

These RAND conference proceedings summarize key issues and topics from the May 11, 2011, symposium. This document is not intended to be a transcript. Rather, it provides an overview of the major themes of discussion by topic, with a particular focus on areas of participants' agreement and disagreement. With the exception of three invited white papers that were written in advance and presented by symposium participants, these proceedings do not attribute remarks to particular individuals. The U.S. Securities and Exchange Commission (SEC) issued final rules implementing the Dodd-Frank whistleblower provisions on May 25, 2011. The authors of the papers included here were given the opportunity to amend their papers accordingly and to comment briefly on the final rules.

These proceedings should be of interest to policymakers, regulators, corporate directors and executives, compliance and ethics practitioners, shareholders, and other stakeholders with an interest in corporate governance, ethics, and compliance practice issues, both in the United States and abroad.

THE RAND CENTER FOR CORPORATE ETHICS AND GOVERNANCE

The Center for Corporate Ethics and Governance is committed to improving public understanding of corporate ethics, law, and governance and to identifying specific ways that businesses can operate ethically, legally, and profitably at the same time. The center's work is supported by voluntary contributions from private-sector organizations and individuals with interests in research on these topics.

The center is part of the RAND Institute for Civil Justice (ICJ), which is dedicated to improving private and public decisionmaking on civil legal issues by supplying policymakers with the results of objective, empirically based, analytic research. The ICJ facilitates change in the civil justice system by analyzing trends and outcomes, identifying and evaluating policy options, and bringing together representatives of different interests to debate alternative solutions to policy problems. ICJ builds on a long tradition of RAND research characterized by an interdisciplinary, empirical approach to public policy issues and rigorous standards of quality, objectivity, and independence.

ICJ research is supported by pooled grants from corporations, trade and professional associations, and individuals; by government grants and contracts; and by private foundations. ICJ disseminates its work widely to the legal, business, and research communities and to the general public. In accordance with RAND policy, all ICJ research products are subject to peer review before publication. ICJ publications do not necessarily reflect the opinions or policies of the research sponsors or of the ICJ Board of Overseers.

Jim Dertouzos, Director
RAND Institute for Civil Justice
1776 Main Street
P.O. Box 2138
Santa Monica, CA 90407–2138
310-393–0411 x7476
Fax: 310-451-6979
James_Dertouzos@rand.org

Michael Greenberg, Director
Center for Corporate Ethics and Governance
4570 Fifth Avenue, Suite 600
Pittsburgh, PA 15213-2665
412-683-2300 x4648
Fax: 412-683-2800
Email: Michael_Greenberg@rand.org

CONTENTS

SUMMARY

In July 2010, President Barack Obama signed into law the Dodd-Frank Wall Street Reform and Consumer Protection Act, a lengthy statute that included a new mechanism for offering bounties to internal corporate "whistleblowers" who report instances of fraud to the SEC. Under the statute, such whistleblowers are entitled to an award (or "bounty") of between 10 and 30 percent of any penalties or fees imposed in amounts greater than $1 million. The SEC released a corresponding set of proposed whistleblower rules in November 2010 and, following a period of notice and comment, promulgated the final whistleblower rules on May 25, 2011. Perhaps the single most contentious feature of the new Dodd-Frank whistleblower regime is that the rules do *not* require that a corporate insider first make use of his or her company's internal reporting channels as a prerequisite for access to the SEC and any potential award under Dodd-Frank.

The notions of Dodd-Frank awards and direct reporting to the SEC have been very controversial in the corporate community, raising concerns about opportunistic claims and the possibility that the new incentives could have the effect of sabotaging internal compliance in many organizations. Whistleblower advocates, on the other hand, have suggested that these fears are likely overblown and are contradicted by empirical data on analogous whistleblower litigation and claimants under the (longstanding) False Claims Act. The debate over the merits of the Dodd-Frank whistleblower scheme, and its likely impact on corporations, overshadows a deeper set of questions for policymakers and the corporate community—questions about how best to prevent corporate fraud and misconduct, how robust most companies' internal compliance and reporting mechanisms truly are, and how best to reconcile internal reporting, compliance, and ethical corporate culture with the new reality of whistleblower awards under Dodd-Frank.

It was in this context that RAND convened a May 11, 2011, symposium, titled "For Whom the Whistle Blows: Corporate Whistleblowing, Federal Policy, and the Shifting Landscape of Corporate Compliance and Culture." The aim of the symposium was to stimulate a broad conversation about the Dodd-Frank whistleblower provisions and about internal reporting and compliance oversight mechanisms within corporations. The symposium brought together a group of 20 senior thought leaders, drawing from the ranks of public company directors and executives, chief ethics and compliance officers (CECOs), and stakeholders from the government, industry, academic, and nonprofit sectors. Discussions focused on the probable impact of the new whistleblower rules on corporate America; the importance of internal compliance and reporting efforts to corporations, regulators, and employees alike; and concrete steps that could be taken to make organizational compliance and internal reporting mechanisms stronger in the era of Dodd-Frank.

Several major themes emerged from the symposium discussions. The first was the observation that employees are a prime resource for detecting corporate fraud and that they can be a major asset to their own companies in that regard. This being said, it is often difficult to convince employees to come forward and report misconduct and fraud internally, in part because of concerns about confidentially, the potential for management retaliation, and skepticism about whether management will act upon any reports received. These are problems with internal reporting that can and should be addressed, regardless of Dodd-Frank. A second general theme focused on ways to help deconflict internal reporting mechanisms and the Dodd-Frank whistleblower channel so that the former can be made maximally effective while use of the latter is minimized. The joint interests of the corporate community and the SEC are likely to be well served by this kind of "deconflicting," to the extent reasonably practical. A third broad symposium theme highlighted the heightened incentive, in the era of Dodd-Frank, for companies to create an organizational culture in which employees can raise concerns safely within the organization. The goal is to make the internal reporting line the insider's mechanism of choice. In this context, the group discussed the critical role of an empowered, senior-level chief compliance officer to oversee the compliance program and internal reporting system. In a related vein, the group also discussed the use of financial and non-financial incentives in connection with a variety of anti-fraud and corporate compliance goals.

INVITED REMARKS FROM FOUR PANELISTS

The initial session of the symposium was dedicated to invited remarks from four panelists who (respectively) represented the viewpoints of corporate defense counsel, whistleblower advocate, and CECO with regard to the impact and implications of the Dodd-Frank whistleblower rules. The speakers were Steven Pearlman, a partner at Seyfarth Shaw LLP; Stephen Kohn, executive director of the National Whistleblowers Center; Patrick Gnazzo, senior vice president and general manager for the U.S. public sector at CA Technologies (retired); and Joseph Murphy, public policy chair at the Society of Corporate Compliance and Ethics and Of Counsel at the Compliance Systems Legal Group (retired). Their remarks were based on invited white papers on the following topics (respectively): "New Whistleblower Policies and Incentives: A Paradigm Shift from 'Oversight' to 'Insight,'" "The Impact of Qui Tam Whistleblower Rewards on Internal Compliance," and "An Insider Perspective on Whistleblower Programs." (The third paper was co-authored by Gnazzo and Murphy.) The three invited white papers were distributed to symposium participants in advance of the meeting on May 11 to set context and facilitate a dynamic discussion.

EXPLORING THE NEW WORLD ORDER: WHISTLEBLOWER CHALLENGES FOR CORPORATE MANAGEMENT AND GOVERNANCE

The second session of the symposium involved a moderated discussion of the challenges posed by the new whistleblower regime under Dodd-Frank, particularly the incentives for direct reporting of fraud by corporate insiders to the SEC. The session opened with some reflections on the problems that have long confronted internal corporate compliance and reporting programs and that often cause the programs to fall short of their expected goals of preventing and detecting misconduct. The question was raised: How much difference will Dodd-Frank and the new whistleblower incentives truly make to internal compliance efforts? Notably, it was observed that boards and senior management already face some of the same basic problems in promoting effective internal compliance and reporting, regardless of the Dodd-Frank whistleblower rules. It was also observed that differences of opinion over the new whistleblower roles tie back, in part, to perceptions of how well current corporate compliance mechanisms are actually working. Critics of the rules tend to view internal compliance efforts as adequate but broadly threatened by the prospect of whistleblower bounties and direct reporting to the SEC, whereas advocates for the Dodd-Frank rules tend to view existing internal compliance efforts and reporting channels as inadequate or insubstantial in too many instances.

The session's opening remarks also underscored the importance of improving the ways in which companies manage their internal reporting mechanisms—encouraging adequate resourcing, board-level oversight, more consistent and professional investigation protocols, and more meaningful protection of internal whistleblowers from retaliation—all of which require strong, independent leadership in the role of the CECO. Participants noted that this is a key set of issues to consider in making internal corporate reporting more robust and in reducing the attractiveness of an external whistleblowing pathway for employees.

Some of the ensuing discussions touched on the specific role of boards in dealing with whistleblower issues, the responsibilities of the CECO and how that particular management role relates to whistleblower issues, and the connection between whistleblowing (whether internal or external) and corporate culture. The reality that corporate misbehavior and ethically dubious conduct remain serious problems in the United States and abroad, despite widespread awareness and recent scandals, was also a significant theme of conversation. Session participants generally agreed on several points:

- Boards of directors play an important role in reinforcing internal reporting mechanisms and ethical culture.
- Empowered leadership for internal reporting, in the form of a senior-level, experienced CECO, is vital to the success of compliance and ethics (C&E) programs and internal reporting mechanisms.
- Creating a culture in which internal reporting is valued—and in which those who report are protected—is critical to preventing and detecting misconduct internally.
- Financial and non-financial incentives could be used by corporations to make internal corporate reporting mechanisms more effective.
- From the perspective of the employee, trust in the system is a key motivator in coming forward and reporting internally.

CORPORATE INTEGRITY IN THE WAKE OF DODD-FRANK: HOW DO WE FORTIFY INTERNAL COMPLIANCE, REPORTING, AND CULTURE?

Participants in the final session of the symposium focused more deeply on the aim of reinforcing corporate compliance efforts and culture and on policy and practice interventions that could help companies accomplish this goal. Introductory remarks during this session observed that even if a corporation's compliance and internal reporting mechanisms initially work well, these efforts can erode over time (and through subsequent generations of management) when there is a lack of abiding institutional commitment behind them. Questions were raised about the best ways to use financial and non-financial incentives to support lasting C&E performance and about the potential for regulatory policies that might support managers in the CECO role in establishing a more aggressive anti-retaliatory posture. It was emphasized again that the ultimate strategy for strengthening internal reporting mechanisms involves embedding these mechanisms in a broader corporate "culture of integrity," in which employees recognize themselves as accountable for safeguarding the reputation of the company and in which they feel protected and encouraged in coming forward to report instances of wrongdoing or misconduct. Much of the discussion in this session touched on the public policy avenues for supporting stronger corporate culture and internal compliance efforts and for reconciling that support with the new external whistleblowing framework established under Dodd-Frank.

The major points of discussion and agreement during the session included the following:

- New requirements for C&E expertise on boards and on key board and executive committees should be considered.
- The SEC should publicize more regulatory data in support of strong compliance efforts and offer incentives to create a robust and independent CECO role.
- Tangible steps can be taken to reinforce C&E and internal reporting lines, such as addressing employees' fears about retaliation and ineffective follow-through.
- Internal reporting and external whistleblowing need not be viewed as antithetical and mutually exclusive.
- Ongoing dialogue between the compliance community and the SEC can help facilitate more effective internal and external reporting processes and, thus, better compliance efforts in the future.

ACKNOWLEDGMENTS

I wish to thank the panelists, speakers, and all those who participated in the roundtable discussions, without whom the exchange of ideas documented here would not have been possible. I would also like to thank our premier sponsor, EthicsPoint, and our supporting sponsor, Seyfarth Shaw LLP, for their generous support of the symposium event. I particularly thank the invited white paper authors who spoke at the symposium: Steven Pearlman, Stephen Kohn, Patrick Gnazzo, and Joseph Murphy. Harold Tinkler and Keith Darcy also made notable contributions to the conversation, as did Stephen Cohen, Sean McKessy, and James Thomson. A full list of participants and their affiliations can be found in Appendix A. Acting as my symposium co-chair, Donna Boehme provided invaluable contributions in structuring and facilitating the discussions and in helping to bring the right group of people to the conference table.

Finally, I would also like to thank Amy Coombe, Michelle Horner, and Jamie Morikawa at RAND for their assistance in organizing the symposium event, managing logistics, capturing the discussions on the day of the event, and generating these proceedings.

Quis custodiet ipsos custodes?

ABBREVIATIONS

ACFE	Association of Certified Fraud Examiners
C&E	compliance and ethics
CECO	chief ethics and compliance officer
CEO	chief executive officer
ERC	Ethics Resource Center
FCA	False Claims Act
ICJ	RAND Institute for Civil Justice
IRS	Internal Revenue Service
NWC	National Whistleblowers Center
OECD	Organisation for Economic Co-Operation and Development
SEC	U.S. Securities and Exchange Commission
SOX	Sarbanes-Oxley Act of 2002
USSC	U.S. Sentencing Commission

1. INTRODUCTION

In July 2010, President Barack Obama signed into law the Dodd-Frank Wall Street Reform and Consumer Protection Act (Pub. L. 111-203), a lengthy statute that included a new mechanism for offering bounties to internal corporate "whistleblowers" who report instances of fraud to the U.S. Securities and Exchange Commission (SEC). Under the statute, such whistleblowers are entitled to receive between 10 and 30 percent of any penalties or fees imposed in amounts greater than $1 million. The new provisions under Dodd-Frank represent a major expansion on earlier pieces of legislation that established whistleblower incentive schemes, most notably including the federal False Claims Act (FCA). The Dodd-Frank provisions also represent a departure from the Sarbanes-Oxley Act of 2002 (SOX), which aimed to encourage more reporting by insiders of securities law violations but did so primarily through anti-retaliation measures and mandates for internal reporting mechanisms. The new whistleblower provisions under Dodd-Frank have been controversial, due in part to fears that internal compliance within firms might be sabotaged as a result. The controversy was especially pronounced after the SEC released its proposed rules in November 2010, in which the commission declined to make access to whistleblower bounties contingent on first reporting instances of misconduct internally within a company.

Critics of the whistleblower rules under Dodd-Frank assert a litany of ill effects that they believe will accrue under the law. As outlined in the recent congressional testimony of Ken Daly, president of the National Association of Corporate Directors, the potential for enormous bounties might lead corporate insiders to let instances of fraud go undetected without reporting them internally, only to later bring them directly to the SEC in the hopes of securing a large financial award.[1] Similar concerns were expressed by the U.S. Chamber of Commerce and others, who cautioned that some aspects of the Dodd-Frank rules might "undermine the functioning of effective corporate compliance programs by relegating them to the sidelines in the process of identifying and remedying violations of securities laws."[2] Both the National Association of Corporate Directors and the Chamber of Commerce took the position that corporate employees ought to be required to report instances of suspected fraud internally within their companies as a condition for subsequent eligibility for whistleblower bounties under Dodd-Frank. And as one commentator recently observed, future SEC enforcement actions (particularly under the Foreign Corrupt Practices Act) make the possibility of future high-value whistleblower payouts seem likely. "Then the floodgates will truly open."[3]

---

[1] See Daly, 2011.
[2] See U.S. Chamber of Commerce et al., 2010, p. 4.
[3] See Clark, 2010.

A contrasting viewpoint has been offered by advocates from the whistleblower community. According to results from the latest iteration of the National Business Ethics Survey, the prevalence of observed misconduct in the corporate workplace remains widespread, yet more than 40 percent of those occurrences are never disclosed to anyone by the witnessing employees. Of those instances that are disclosed by an employee, most are reported directly to an immediate supervisor and not via a formal compliance mechanism.[4] In a somewhat different vein, recent empirical studies of successful *qui tam* claimants under the FCA suggest that a substantial majority actually do try to report misconduct internally within their own companies and only blow the whistle as a last course of action.[5] These kinds of findings illustrate a basic tension in the ways in which different people view the corporate compliance function.

Among many executives and directors in the business community, compliance programs are viewed as basically effective *ex ante* and threatened by new external whistleblower awards. Some whistleblower advocates and other commentators, on the other hand, suggest the opposite—that many employees lack trust in internal compliance and reporting channels and that most would be only too happy to use them if they felt safer and better protected in doing so. A complementary observation has been put forward by some leading members of the compliance profession—namely, in too many corporations, compliance and ethics programs are either broken or hollow, and much more needs to be done to make those programs truly effective.[6] In a 2009 RAND symposium, significant discussion focused on the lack of a strong, independent chief ethics and compliance officer (CECO) as a key indicium of a weak or failing program. As the author of one invited white paper opined, "A well-implemented compliance and ethics program doesn't spring from the void ex nihilo—it requires a strong leader to engage others in the organization, including powerful senior managers, to surface and resolve issues and challenges, and to make a culture of transparency, accountability and responsibility a reality."[7]

The debate over whistleblowing under Dodd-Frank invokes radically different viewpoints about the psychology of employees who come forward to reveal misconduct. Is the decision to report primarily opportunistic and strongly motivated by perceptions about the potential for large financial reward? Or is the decision inherently risky, such that a person's career, family, and home may be placed in jeopardy by coming forward? Without seeking an objective answer to these competing visions, it is important to recognize that the Dodd-Frank

---

[4] See Ethics Resource Center, 2010.

[5] See, e.g., Kesselheim, Studdert, and Mello, 2010. According to *Black's Law Dictionary* (1990, p. 1251), "Qui Tam is an action brought by an informer, under a statute which establishes a penalty for the commission or omission of a certain act, and provides that the same shall be recoverable in a civil action, part of the penalty to go to any person who will bring such action and the remainder to the state or to some other institution."

[6] See Greenberg, 2009.

[7] See Boehme, 2009, pp. 28–29.

regime is premised on the idea that both viewpoints may simultaneously be true. In other words, incentives for whistleblowing may be desirable precisely because it is difficult, risky, and unpalatable for employees to come forward, and it is frequently easier for them simply to remain silent. Meanwhile, are employees' decisions about external whistleblowing likely to be influenced by access to robust internal reporting mechanisms, together with a culture of ethics and trust in the workplace? This is a nebulous question to try to address with empirical data. It seems intuitive, though, that a hypothetical stampede of whistleblower claims under Dodd-Frank might more likely occur in a world in which instances of corporate fraud and opportunistic behavior are widespread, internal compliance mechanisms are not trustworthy, and commitments to honesty and fair dealing are not viewed as basic attributes of the corporation or the employment relationship.

In some basic sense, the superficial debate over whether the Dodd-Frank whistleblower provisions are a good idea conceals some underlying points of broad agreement. Corporate fraud and misconduct are bad things. Compliance and ethics programs are intended to protect companies themselves, as well as the community at large, from bad behavior. An ideal world is one in which the occurrence of misconduct in corporations is low, in which employees trust internal reporting mechanisms, and in which those mechanisms make external whistleblowing largely superfluous. These are points that reflect the shared interest of the corporate community, regulators, and employees and that move beyond the basic debate over government bounties and external whistleblowing. That debate has largely been rendered moot by the final SEC whistleblower rules under Dodd-Frank, which were promulgated in May 2011 and establish that internal reporting of fraud is not required for subsequent eligibility for an SEC whistleblower award. Given the new reality of the external whistleblower rules, the key question for all stakeholders becomes, How can internal reporting mechanisms and compliance and ethics (C&E) programs broadly be made more effective, in a way that minimizes the need for external whistleblowing? Furthermore, are there ways to ensure that the corporate community and regulators can work together toward this end and that compliance programs are neither sabotaged nor "bumped to the sidelines" by Dodd-Frank?

It was in this context that RAND convened a May 11, 2011, symposium event, titled "For Whom the Whistle Blows: Corporate Whistleblowing, Federal Policy, and the Shifting Landscape of Corporate Compliance and Culture." The aim of the symposium was to stimulate a broad conversation about the Dodd-Frank whistleblower provisions and about internal reporting and compliance oversight mechanisms within corporations. The symposium also sought to build on previous RAND-organized roundtable meetings that focused on the roles of chief compliance officers and corporate boards in helping to meet C&E challenges within firms.[8] The May 2011 symposium brought together a group of 20 senior thought leaders, drawing from the ranks of public company directors and executives, CECOs, and stakeholders from the

---

[8] See Greenberg, 2009, 2010.

government, academic, and nonprofit sectors. Discussions focused on the probable impact of the new whistleblower rules on corporate America; the importance of internal compliance and reporting efforts to corporations, regulators, and employees alike; and concrete steps that could be taken to make compliance and internal reporting mechanisms stronger in the wake of Dodd-Frank. Participants in the May 2011 RAND symposium are listed in Appendix A of this document, and the conference agenda is reproduced in Appendix B.

Prior to the symposium, four of the invited participants were asked to prepare and present formal remarks on the Dodd-Frank whistleblower provisions, representing the varied perspectives of outside corporate litigation counsel, whistleblower advocate, and corporate ethics and compliance officer. These remarks were then presented in the initial session of the conference. A short summary of the speakers' remarks is presented in Chapter Two; the papers on which these remarks were based are reproduced in their entirety in Appendix C of this document.

The second session of the symposium involved a moderated discussion on the topic of "Exploring the New World Order: Whistleblower Challenges for Corporate Management and Governance." Chapter Three provides a summary of the major themes and topics of conversation in this session.

The final session of the symposium involved a moderated discussion on the topic of "Corporate Integrity in the Wake of Dodd-Frank: How Do We Fortify Internal Compliance, Reporting, and Culture?" Chapter Four provides a summary of major themes and ideas that were discussed in this session.

2. INVITED REMARKS FROM SYMPOSIUM PARTICIPANTS

OVERVIEW

The symposium began with remarks from four of the participants in attendance: Steven Pearlman, a partner at Seyfarth Shaw LLP; Stephen Kohn, executive director of the National Whistleblowers Center; Patrick Gnazzo, senior vice president and general manager for the U.S. public sector at CA Technologies (retired); and Joseph Murphy, public policy chair at the Society of Corporate Compliance and Ethics and Of Counsel at the Compliance Systems Legal Group (retired). Their remarks were based on invited white papers on the respective topics of "New Whistleblower Policies and Incentives: A Paradigm Shift from 'Oversight' to 'Insight,'" "The Impact of *Qui Tam* Whistleblower Rewards on Internal Compliance," and "An Insider Perspective on Whistleblower Programs." (The third paper was co-authored by Gnazzo and Murphy.) Each author and topic was selected to bring an important expert viewpoint to, and set the context for, the symposium discussions. This chapter presents brief summaries of each set of remarks. The invited white papers are reproduced in their entirety in Appendix C.

SUMMARY:
NEW WHISTLEBLOWER POLICIES AND INCENTIVES:
A PARADIGM SHIFT FROM "*OVER*SIGHT" TO "*IN*SIGHT"

Steven J. Pearlman, Seyfarth Shaw LLP

The new Dodd-Frank whistleblower provision (Pub. L. 111-203, Sec. 922) represents a major departure from previous federal whistleblower policies with regard to corporate fraud and wrongdoing. For public companies going forward, understanding the contours of the new Dodd-Frank whistleblower law will be important in mitigating risk. For policymakers, the new law invites questions about whether public and investor interests are truly well served by injecting a bounty hunter mentality into the workplace.

Whistleblower Bounty Provision Under Dodd Frank

Section 922 of Dodd-Frank provides that a whistleblower may be eligible for a bounty of between 10 and 30 percent of the SEC's recovery if she or he voluntarily provides original information to the SEC that leads to the successful enforcement of a federal court or administrative action in which the SEC obtains monetary sanctions totaling more than $1 million. Neither the statute nor the SEC rules require employees to complain internally before blowing the whistle to the SEC.

Charting the Impact of Dodd-Frank on the Legal Landscape

Section 922 of Dodd-Frank represents a paradigm shift from "*over*sight" to "*in*sight" when contrasted with previous whistleblower policy under SOX. The earlier legislation notably included whistleblower anti-retaliation as one part of a mandate for stronger corporate compliance mechanisms, comprising anonymous reporting procedures, independent audit committees, internal financial controls, and formal codes of ethics and conduct. Taken together, the effect of the SOX provisions was to incentivize and strengthen internal compliance efforts within firms. The new Dodd-Frank provision, by contrast, is likely to have the opposite effect: It will undermine internal compliance efforts by encouraging employees to circumvent internal reporting procedures and to go directly to the SEC with allegations of securities law violations.

Section 922 of Dodd-Frank dramatically expands on the scope of earlier federal *qui tam* provisions, such as the FCA, the Internal Revenue Service (IRS) whistleblower law, and the SEC's legacy insider-trading rule.

What Are the Implications of Whistleblower Bounties Under Dodd Frank?

The new Dodd-Frank whistleblower provision is likely to have perverse and negative consequences for firms and investors in a variety of areas:

- Employees with information about fraud or misconduct will now have an incentive to allow problems to grow without reporting them internally so that the SEC's eventual recovery, and any corresponding whistleblower bounty, will be greater.
- Because employees have a strong incentive to report directly to the SEC, companies will be deprived of opportunities to conduct prompt internal investigations and to take remedial measures when instances of fraud do occur.
- Bounty-hunter incentives are likely to erode trust between management and employees, compromise employee relations, and exert a chilling effect on broader information sharing within organizations.
- The potential for very large (multimillion-dollar) bounty awards could easily result in a blizzard of frivolous or underdeveloped whistleblower claims, which is likely to be self-defeating for regulators and highly disruptive for firms.

For policymakers, the key question going forward is whether the ill effects of the Dodd-Frank whistleblower provisions outweigh any putative enforcement gains that might accrue from the statute. For firms, the key question will be how to operate effectively in the new Dodd-Frank environment and how to protect internal compliance mechanisms from erosion under Dodd-Frank's influence.

SUMMARY:
THE IMPACT OF *QUI TAM* WHISTLEBLOWER REWARDS ON INTERNAL COMPLIANCE

Stephen Martin Kohn, National Whistleblowers Center

The new Dodd-Frank whistleblower provision serves the public interest by creating policies to encourage the reporting of suspected violations of law within corporations to appropriate authorities. The new law responds directly to empirical evidence showing that insider tips are the single most important resource for detecting fraud. Similar whistleblower provisions (particularly under the FCA) have proved to be very effective in generating major civil returns to government and in creating new incentives for federal contractors to prevent fraud. Fears about the potential negative impact of Dodd-Frank on internal compliance programs are overblown and contradicted by empirical data suggesting that most whistleblowers actually do try to report internally, prior to any pursuit of outside whistleblower claims.

Employee Reporting Behavior

In a recent review of more than 1,800 cases of corporate fraud, the Association of Certified Fraud Examiners (ACFE) 2010 Global Fraud Study found that inside tips accounted for the detection of fraud in more than 40 percent of the cases studied. The ACFE study also found that inside tips were the single most prevalent method of fraud detection and were as important as the next three most common methods of detecting fraud combined. Meanwhile, recent survey findings from the Ethics Resource Center (ERC) indicate that workplace fraud and misconduct remain highly prevalent—and that many instances of fraud are never reported by employees to anyone. According to the ERC, the vast majority of employees who do report fraud do not go to law-enforcement authorities but instead to their own supervisors or higher management in their own firms. The ERC concluded that the failure of employees to report misconduct continues to present a major problem, one that has an impact on the effectiveness of both internal corporate compliance programs and government law-enforcement efforts.

Qui Tam Success Under the False Claims Act and the Impact on Internal Compliance

The success of whistleblower reporting under the FCA has been well documented in statistics published by the U.S. Department of Justice. Civil fines and penalties obtained by the United States have risen dramatically in the decades since the FCA whistleblower rule was enacted, with billions of dollars in recoveries associated with illegal contracting and procurement practices. Moreover, there is reason to believe that these statistics undervalue the true deterrence and anti-fraud contribution made by whistleblowers, especially since settlement agreements in *qui tam* cases often include extensive compliance requirements imposed on the companies that enter into them.

Meanwhile, empirical evidence contradicts the most serious argument typically asserted against whistleblower *qui tam* provisions—namely, that such laws encourage employees to ignore internal reporting processes in favor of seeking bounties from outside authorities. Recent studies by the National Whistleblowers Center and others suggest that the vast majority of employees who eventually go on to file *qui tam* claims initially attempt to resolve their disputes via internal channels within their own companies. Moreover, only a tiny fraction of *qui tam* claimants actually work within the corporate compliance function. These sorts of empirical findings about whistleblowers suggest that the argument that Dodd-Frank will lead to a massive new wave of employee claims is considerably overblown.

Narrow Interpretation of Anti-Retaliation Statutes Has Probably Been More Damaging to Internal Compliance Efforts

For decades, corporate counsel have argued emphatically that anti-retaliation provisions under whistleblower laws do *not* apply to employee reporting through internal compliance programs. A long string of federal precedents, beginning with *Brown & Root v. Donovan* (1984), bears witness to arguments by corporate counsel to limit the reach of whistleblower anti-retaliation provisions and to court rulings that construed internal reporting as beyond the scope of what "whistleblower" anti-retaliation is supposed to protect. These sorts of rulings are likely far more damaging to internal compliance efforts than are *qui tam* incentives, especially given empirical data suggesting that underreporting of corporate misconduct continues to be a serious problem.

Recommendations

In sum, empirical and historical evidence suggests the following:

- The overwhelming majority of employees utilize internal reporting procedures, despite the existence *qui tam* provisions and the potential for monetary rewards.
- The existence of whistleblower rewards has no negative impact on the performance of compliance personnel, who themselves account for only a tiny fraction of whistleblower claimants.
- Whistleblower reward programs are highly effective in assisting in the detection of fraud and the enforcement of anti-corruption laws.

Based on the foregoing, there is a strong argument that whistleblower reward programs should actually be expanded rather than curtailed and, in particular, that corporations should consider initiating internal reward programs to strengthen their compliance efforts.

SUMMARY:
AN INSIDER PERSPECTIVE ON WHISTLEBLOWER PROGRAMS

Patrick Gnazzo, CA Technologies (Retired), and
Joseph Murphy, Society of Corporate Compliance and Ethics, and Of Counsel, Compliance
Systems Legal Group (Retired)

Role of the Internal Employee Reporting Program

Internal whistleblowers received a significant boost with the adoption of the Federal Sentencing Guidelines for Organizations in 1991, when the U.S. Sentencing Commission established that an internal reporting system was a key element in an effective compliance program and a factor to be considered in sentencing leniency under the guidelines. In the decades since, major corporations have tended to implement helplines under the supervision of their CECOs, who use those lines to drive internal investigations and to report results to top management and boards. In short, internal company reporting systems have become a near-global policy as part of the effort to prevent corporate crime and ethical misconduct.

Controversy: The Impact of Dodd-Frank Whistleblower Rules on Internal Programs

Many in the corporate community see in Dodd-Frank the potential to undermine internal compliance programs. Managers fear that employees will circumvent internal reporting channels in a race to obtain bounties, or that external *qui tam* claims will delay or derail internal investigations. These fears merit serious consideration, even though past studies on *qui tam* belie the argument that whistleblowers are primarily motivated by the prospect of financial gain. Rather, the most important impediment to internal reporting by employees tends to be the perception that nobody is really listening. This is a key problem for companies seeking to minimize *qui tam* risk.

Pros and Cons of Internal Helplines

Many helplines do not work as intended. For internal reporting systems to operate effectively, implementation, non-retaliation, and effective follow-up are crucial. The best way to ensure that these steps are taken is to appoint an empowered senior-level CECO—one with the mandate, experience, positioning, and resources to develop and oversee an effective compliance program. This recommendation is much in line with the standards articulated by the Federal Sentencing Guidelines for Organizations and the 2010 Organisation for Economic Co-Operation and Development (OECD) Good Practice Guidance on Internal Controls, Ethics and Compliance.

Both Government Whistleblowing and Internal Reporting Lines Have Drawbacks

Public-sector whistleblower mechanisms cannot replace internal compliance and reporting systems. Whistleblower laws and enforcement mechanisms are subject to some fundamental limitations and weaknesses:

1. They can take a very long time to resolve claims.
2. Government resources are limited, so small claims may be considered low-priority.
3. The employee's name typically becomes evident, and, for the most part, his or her career is ended.
4. If the organization is not found guilty or does not settle, the whistleblower receives nothing.

This being said, there are some limitations and downsides associated with internal employee reporting lines as well:

1. Employees may not believe that any action will be taken.
2. Employees may not trust the protection promised by the organization.
3. It is difficult to investigate an allegation that comes in anonymously, especially when not enough facts are brought forward by the anonymous employee.
4. An employee who remains anonymous never receives recognition or compensation for coming forward to protect the organization.

Despite these limitations, internal employee helplines establish a basic corporate commitment to reporting and to incentives that discourage fraud and misconduct.

How Government and Companies Can Work Together to Prevent and Detect Corporate Wrongdoing and to Support Both Internal and External Whistleblower Programs

The SEC has attempted to strike a balance in its proposed rule-making under Dodd-Frank between protecting strong internal compliance programs and providing direct access to federal whistleblower incentives and protections when internal programs fail. Some additional ways in which the SEC and companies could work together to improve the balance include the following:

1. Establish a protocol for SEC discretionary referral of Dodd-Frank whistleblower matters to companies/CECOs for initial investigation, including matters to be considered for investigation and criteria, standards, and processes for company eligibility.
2. Make clear that companies that show diligence in their commitment to C&E will benefit from leniency in the SEC's enforcement decisions under Dodd-Frank.

3. Establish a protocol for determining eligibility for lenient treatment, based on a C&E program linked to an empowered CECO, that includes standards for determining whether a company has an empowered CECO.

4. Form an informal C&E working group that includes experienced CECOs, facilitated by a credible nonprofit organization, to address these matters on an ongoing basis.

5. Review other steps that the SEC can take to encourage stronger company C&E programs (e.g., specifically include such efforts in the SEC's penalty policy, provide more detail on the role of C&E programs in enforcement decisions).

3. EXPLORING THE NEW WORLD ORDER: WHISTLEBLOWER CHALLENGES FOR CORPORATE MANAGEMENT AND GOVERNANCE

OVERVIEW

Participants in this session of the symposium discussed a broad range of challenges posed by the new whistleblower regime under Dodd-Frank, particularly by incentives for direct reporting of fraud by corporate insiders to the SEC. The session opened with some reflections on the problems that have long confronted internal corporate compliance and reporting programs—and that often cause the programs to fall short in meeting expected goals of preventing and detecting misconduct. The question was raised: How much difference will Dodd-Frank and the new whistleblower incentives truly make to internal compliance efforts? Notably, it was observed that boards and senior management already face some of the same basic problems in promoting effective internal compliance and reporting, regardless of the Dodd-Frank whistleblower rules. It was also observed that differences of opinion over the new whistleblower roles tie back, in part, to perceptions of how well current corporate compliance mechanisms are actually working. Critics of the rules tend to view internal compliance efforts as adequate but broadly threatened by the prospect of whistleblower bounties and direct reporting to the SEC, whereas advocates for the Dodd-Frank rules tend to view existing internal compliance efforts and reporting channels as inadequate or insubstantial in too many instances.

On a similar note, the opening remarks for the session also underscored the importance of improving the ways in which companies manage their internal reporting mechanisms—encouraging adequate resourcing, board-level oversight, more consistent and professional investigation protocols, and more meaningful protection of internal whistleblowers from retaliation—all of which require strong, independent leadership in the role of the CECO. Participants observed that this is a key set of issues to consider when making internal corporate reporting more robust and in reducing the attractiveness of or need for an external whistleblowing pathway for employees.

Some of the ensuing discussions touched on the specific role of boards in dealing with whistleblower issues, the independence of the CECO and how that particular management role relates to whistleblower issues, and the connection between whistleblowing (whether internal or external) and corporate culture. The reality that corporate misbehavior and ethically dubious conduct remain serious problems in the United States and abroad, despite widespread awareness and recent scandals, was also a significant theme of conversation. Session participants generally agreed on several points:

- Boards of directors play an important role in reinforcing internal reporting mechanisms and ethical culture.

- Empowered leadership for internal reporting, in the form of a senior-level experienced CECO, is vital to the success of C&E programs and internal reporting mechanisms.
- Creating a culture in which internal reporting is valued—and in which those who report are protected—is critical to preventing and detecting misconduct internally.
- Financial and non-financial incentives could be used by corporations to make internal corporate reporting mechanisms more effective.
- From the perspective of the employee, trust in the system is a key motivator in coming forward and reporting internally.

BOARDS OF DIRECTORS PLAY AN IMPORTANT ROLE IN REINFORCING INTERNAL REPORTING MECHANISMS AND ETHICAL CULTURE

One of the major themes of conversation involved the role of boards of directors in dealing with, supporting, or otherwise responding to corporate whistleblowers. In principle, internal whistleblowers ought to be an important resource to boards and senior management, one that can provide an early warning of instances of material fraud or misconduct within companies. At the same time, concerns about opportunistic whistleblower litigation also rise to the board level, based on fears that such litigation might affect corporate bottom lines, even when specific claims are without merit. The challenges posed by whistleblowers and effective internal reporting arise against a backdrop of boards' increasing responsibility for a range of C&E matters. Recent revisions to the Federal Sentencing Guidelines for Organizations notably emphasized the role of the board and the CECO in contributing to effective corporate compliance.[9] And several major common-law precedents in Delaware, including *In re: Caremark* and *Stone v. Ritter*, have established that corporate boards are at risk for personal liability if they neglect to fulfill a duty of oversight connected with the compliance function. Taken together, these various strands underscore the fact that internal reporting and external whistleblower issues are closely tied to the responsibilities of persons serving in corporate boardrooms.

Several participants in the symposium commented that the perceived independence of the board, and its availability as the ultimate recipient of internal reports of corporate wrongdoing, are important factors contributing to an effective internal reporting process and a strong ethical culture. One participant suggested that visible board-level support for compliance programs and internal reporting conveys a message to corporate employees that "the company cares" and that there is meaningful substance to the internal reporting channel. Others observed that the relationship between the board and the CECO is particularly important in this regard, since the CECO is simultaneously the head of the internal reporting

---

[9] See U.S. Sentencing Commission, 2010, p. 519 (§ 8C2.5). Key language in the revised guidelines notably provides for leniency in sentencing based on an "effective compliance and ethics program," which, in turn, is partly characterized as establishing "direct reporting authority" between the CECO and the board.

mechanism and the conduit for passing related information on allegations and investigations back up to the board level. Several participants commented that the role of the board involves setting a fundamental tone for the corporation with regard to internal reporting. And although this "tone at the top" manifests partly through the selection of the chief executive officer (CEO) and the ethical commitment of individual board members, it is also communicated through board support for the CECO role and the board's level of interest in receiving regular information about the compliance program and internal reporting process.

Other comments during the symposium session tied board involvement in internal reporting to a range of other issues, including appropriate compensation incentives, related performance metrics, and non-retaliation. The board potentially has some involvement in all of these matters, either by contributing to internal policy or by ensuring that appropriate performance data and information are flowing back up to the board. In turn, the board's engagement with these issues contributes to a strong "tone at the top" and the messages conveyed to employees about the fundamental values of the organization (i.e., regarding its "culture"). Ultimately, the discussion about the role of the board also revisited the basic tension over whether the Dodd-Frank whistleblower provisions are a good idea. Although participants continued to express different opinions about this, one of the most striking comments during the session was the suggestion that boards could view the new whistleblower regime as representing an opportunity rather than a catastrophe—an opportunity in which to reinforce the strength of internal reporting mechanisms, to visibly align with anti-corruption and anti-retaliation efforts, and to recognize that employee reporting on fraud is potentially a valuable resource, rather than a threat, to the company.

EMPOWERED LEADERSHIP FOR INTERNAL REPORTING, IN THE FORM OF A SENIOR-LEVEL EXPERIENCED CECO, IS VITAL TO THE SUCCESS OF A C&E PROGRAM AND INTERNAL REPORTING MECHANISMS

Several participants in the session expressed the view that internal reporting is a primary element of effective compliance and, in turn, that the CECO is the driver of both a strong program generally and a robust internal reporting mechanism in particular. It was observed that the CECO is the single person in the company who has the expertise and responsibility to articulate the necessary features of an effective internal reporting program and who can educate and inform both the board and senior management on these issues. The CECO notably serves as the agent of the CEO and the board in heading the internal reporting pipeline and managing related investigations; the CECO can also report findings back to the CEO and the board in a way that protects internal whistleblowers from retaliation. One person commented that the CECO is the visible person at the management level who "stands between the whistleblower and retaliation, without any conflicting duties." Another observed that the term *anti-retaliation* is often perceived as empty by corporate employees, absent the demonstrated commitment of the CECO to standing behind confidential reporting. In the context of allegations of misconduct against powerful figures within management, the CECO role may sometimes involve confronting senior executives to ensure that the confidentiality and integrity of the reporting process is maintained, despite strong pressures to violate it. This is one of the major reasons that the CECO position can be a very challenging one to fulfill and why there is strong policy momentum to create a robust CECO role with "adequate autonomy from management."[10]

Participants in the symposium expressed a range of views about the necessary features of the CECO role. Several participants alluded to the language of the recent OECD guidance, suggesting that a "senior-level, experienced CECO with adequate autonomy from management" is vital to the success of C&E programs and internal reporting mechanisms. Multiple participants also commented on the importance of separating the C&E function from the general counsel's office, suggesting that the risk management responsibility of the general counsel, at times, pulls in a different direction from the compliance role of the CECO—perhaps particularly in dealing with whistleblowers. Another participant offered a different view, however: that compliance responsibility is not necessarily incompatible with the role of general counsel and that the broader challenge for corporations involves managing institutional conflicts of interest around compliance (and whistleblowing) in a nuanced and reasonable way. There was stronger agreement around the table that the head of the compliance function requires direct access to, and oversight by, the board for the internal reporting and anti-retaliation aspects of the role to be truly empowered and to ensure the independence of the overall compliance program. Discussion also touched on the idea that CECO compensation, hiring, and firing ought to involve board-level supervision and involvement to preserve the independence of the CECO role.

One of the other key comments about the CECO role and internal reporting was that the CECO has both practical and cultural importance. On a practical level, the CECO oversees all the mechanics of operating a confidential reporting line, performing investigations, educating employees and executives, and so on. By extension, when the CECO is not sufficiently empowered, experienced, or resourced, the ability of the company to prevent and detect misconduct is likely to be impaired. Meanwhile, on a cultural level, the CECO role demonstrates corporate commitment to the internal reporting process and to genuinely encouraging employees to come forward and report. The practical and cultural aspects of the CECO role are important to building trust and common ethical values in the workplace, and it may be very relevant in modulating the risks associated with external whistleblowing under Dodd-Frank.

---

[10] See U.S. Sentencing Commission, 2010, and OECD, 2010.

CREATING A CULTURE IN WHICH INTERNAL REPORTING IS VALUED, AND IN WHICH THOSE WHO REPORT ARE PROTECTED, IS CRITICAL TO PREVENTING AND DETECTING MISCONDUCT INTERNALLY

Another theme that emerged during the session involved the relationship between reporting and corporate culture and the importance of "getting the culture right" to facilitate reporting efforts. It was observed that the relationship between ethical culture and internal reporting practice is multifaceted and that the success of each depends to some degree on the other. The topic arose initially through an interchange between participants with different views on the likely impact of the Dodd-Frank whistleblower provisions. One person suggested that the prospect of financial awards for direct reporting to the SEC might have an explosive effect on efforts to build a "culture of integrity" within corporations because such awards encourage a mercenary mentality and undermine trust between employees and management. It was further argued that "companies have to clean from within" and that creating an avenue for employees to bypass internal reporting of fraud could have the effect of "detonating" corporate culture. However, a contrasting viewpoint was also expressed—namely, that the availability of the Dodd-Frank whistleblower channel need not be viewed as antithetical to ethical culture and could instead serve as a rallying point for organizations in seeking to build such a culture. The group discussed the new Dodd-Frank whistleblower rules as presenting incentives for companies to "raise their game" and to evaluate the leadership and resources dedicated to their C&E programs, with the aim of making internal reporting mechanisms the natural choice for employees seeking to report misconduct.

Related conversation in the symposium moved rapidly to focus on strong ethical culture as an antecedent for internal reporting. It was noted that the absence of such culture is one of the chief reasons that employees are sometimes reluctant to make use of internal reporting channels. Several participants spoke specifically about the problems of retaliation and a lack of commitment to protecting whistleblowers as fundamental cultural flaws that can undermine internal reporting schemes. One participant described organizational culture as answering the basic question: How does one overcome widespread reticence among employees to step forward and report internally on fraud in the first place? By extension, "culture" involves ensuring the confidentiality and effective investigation of internal reports of misconduct and, at the same time, conveying the commitment to do so as a basic element in the fabric of the organization. Another participant suggested that employees "need to be told that the board cares about [and is committed to supporting] internal reporting on fraud" and that employees "have to be sold on the concept that if they try to report internally, it will be worth it." Both these sentiments were loosely associated with the concept of "culture" and the perception that the lack of a strong culture may be associated with weakness in internal reporting practices.

Two other major points were raised in context. With regard to successful *qui tam* claims under the FCA, more than one person observed that the substantial majority of such claimants actually do try to report fraud internally prior to going to outside authorities but that those attempts prove unsuccessful in one way or another. These sorts of failures in internal reporting might be construed as reflecting cultural problems in the organizations in which they occur. Another commented that the rationale for the external whistleblower channel in Dodd-Frank originates precisely from the perception among some policymakers that internal corporate reporting mechanisms and protections have not been sufficiently robust or successful in getting employees to come forward. In this sense, the new Dodd-Frank rules might be seen as a response to cultural shortcomings in the organization and as a spur to improvement.

FINANCIAL AND NON-FINANCIAL INCENTIVES CAN BE USED BY CORPORATIONS TO MAKE INTERNAL REPORTING MECHANISMS MORE EFFECTIVE

One of the central topics of discussion during the symposium involved the various uses that might be made of financial and non-financial incentives to try to influence employee reporting behavior in different ways. Again, several respondents expressed worry about the potential for invidious impact of SEC financial incentives under the Dodd-Frank whistleblower provisions and the resulting possibility that some employees might circumvent internal reporting channels altogether or passively allow instances of misconduct to proliferate. Others at the symposium, however, commented that such fears are overblown and that historical evidence on whistleblowing and *qui tam* litigation suggests that the vast majority of whistleblowers do try to make use of internal avenues for reporting fraud, prior to going to outside authorities. One participant argued that Dodd-Frank presents less of a challenge to internal reporting mechanisms than does simple skepticism on the part of employees regarding whether the internal reporting pathway is robust and safe to pursue. Another suggested that, ideally, internal and external reporting avenues could be aligned with each other, even if employees do have the option to go directly to the SEC to report instances of fraud. Still another said that the chief problem faced by all whistleblower mechanisms, internal and external, involves getting people to come forward to report fraud when silence is typically easier and presents far less risk to an employee's career.

One suggestion offered to help reinforce internal reporting was that corporate compensation schemes could be tweaked to include a set of ethical leadership criteria for management, thereby supporting a culture in which internal whistleblowers are supported and valued. It was observed that, in much the same way that compensation incentives can be designed to influence behavior based on a range of business performance metrics and individual behaviors, so too can these incentives be structured to support ethical leadership performance among senior and line management. Along these lines, one participant noted that the CEO and key senior executives could receive contingent compensation based on a range of performance metrics tied to ethical leadership, support of the compliance function, and successful efforts to contribute to ethical culture.

Far more controversial was the suggestion that companies might consider offering bounties or bonuses directly to employees for coming forward internally to report allegations of fraud. One participant suggested that management ought to reward good internal whistleblower tips with bonuses, in much the same way that other valuable contributions to the corporate bottom line are rewarded. Another suggested that specific examples of internal reporting can sometimes involve huge contributions to risk management and corporate welfare, adding that employees who contribute in that way should be recognized and celebrated within the company for doing so. Others at the symposium, however, expressed skepticism about whether corporations could (or should) try to compete with the SEC in actually providing direct payments to encourage internal reporting behavior. One participant argued that such payments might themselves be corrosive to corporate culture, confidentiality, and trust within the workplace. It was also observed that non-financial incentives, such as CEO acknowledgement and company recognition, are often more effective in driving ethical culture.

Deep ambivalence toward whistleblower incentive payments (whether made by the SEC or a corporation itself) was expressed in the comments of several symposium participants, who noted that such payments seem "unsavory" or may smack of "paying a rogue to catch a rogue." It was also noted, however, that the public policy for instituting whistleblower incentives has typically been formulated precisely with the latter aim in mind. The success of past whistleblower efforts in combating fraud is arguably demonstrated by the billions of dollars in settlements and damage payments that have been awarded as a result. By loose analogy, one person suggested that some form of internal corporate incentive payments might also serve as a useful tool for reinforcing the internal compliance function and for rooting out corruption within a company.

FROM THE PERSPECTIVE OF THE INTERNAL WHISTLEBLOWER, TRUST IN THE SYSTEM IS A KEY MOTIVATOR TO COME FORWARD

One significant observation shared at the symposium was that employee trust in internal reporting mechanisms, and in the corporate commitment to anti-retaliation, is central to enticing employees to come forward internally with evidence of fraud or misconduct. As one participant remarked, "People will only come forward to report when they have trust in the system." Another said, "Providing avenues to protect the confidentiality of people who report" is an important factor in "overcoming employee reticence . . . and [fears of] retaliation." A third commented that "employees have to be sold on the concept that if they report internally, it will be worth it." Embedded in all these comments was the notion that employee trust in internal reporting may often be hard to come by and that a lack of trust might be part of the explanation for recent survey findings that a substantial fraction of witnessed incidents of workplace misconduct are never disclosed by the witnessing employee to anyone.[11] In a complementary vein, another participant observed that internal reporting can often be risky for employees and that anecdotal reports of firings or other punitive responses toward internal whistleblowers are not uncommon, despite management lip service to anti-retaliation and the anti-retaliation provisions built into SOX and similar laws.

---

[11] See Ethics Resource Center, 2010.

In some basic sense, employee trust in internal reporting and anti-retaliation efforts is a complement to strong organizational culture. If the latter is perceived by employees as lacking or weak, the former is more likely to be found in short supply. On this point, one participant noted that the corporate commitment to anti-retaliation has sometimes been inconsistent or ambivalent, as reflected in a series of high-profile court cases in which corporations successfully argued that statutory anti-retaliation provisions do not and should not protect employees who make use of internal reporting mechanisms. It was also asserted that these precedents have had the effect of weakening internal reporting channels and simultaneously making corporations look less sincere in their commitment to anti-retaliation. One putative result has been a loss of trust among employees. As another participant put it, whistleblowers "serve a critical purpose" in corporate efforts to self-police against fraud. By extension, protecting confidentiality and fostering trust in internal reporting are key steps for making whistleblowers a corporate asset rather than a threat to the company.

4. CORPORATE INTEGRITY IN THE WAKE OF DODD-FRANK: HOW DO WE FORTIFY INTERNAL COMPLIANCE, REPORTING, AND CULTURE?

OVERVIEW

Participants in the final session of the symposium focused more deeply on the aim of reinforcing corporate compliance efforts and culture and on policy and practice interventions that could help companies accomplish this goal. Introductory remarks during this session observed that even if a corporation's compliance and internal reporting mechanisms initially work well, these efforts can erode over time (and through subsequent generations of management) when there is a lack of abiding institutional commitment behind them. Questions were raised about the best ways to use financial and non-financial incentives to support lasting C&E performance and about the potential for regulatory policies that might support managers in the CECO role in establishing a more aggressive anti-retaliatory posture. It was emphasized again that the ultimate strategy for strengthening internal reporting mechanisms involves embedding these mechanisms in a broader corporate "culture of integrity," in which employees recognize themselves as accountable for safeguarding the reputation of the company and in which they feel protected and encouraged in coming forward to report instances of wrongdoing or misconduct. Much of the discussion in this session touched on the public policy avenues for supporting stronger corporate culture and internal compliance efforts and for reconciling that support with the new external whistleblowing framework established under Dodd-Frank.

Several of the major points of discussion and agreement during the session included the following:

- New requirements for C&E expertise on boards and on key board and executive committees should be considered.
- The SEC should publicize more regulatory data in support of strong compliance efforts and offer incentives to create a robust CECO role.
- Tangible steps can be taken to reinforce C&E and internal reporting lines, such as addressing employee fears about retaliation and ineffective follow-through.
- Internal reporting and external whistleblowing need not be viewed as antithetical and mutually exclusive.
- Ongoing dialogue between the compliance community and the SEC can help facilitate more effective internal and external reporting processes and, thus, better compliance efforts in the future.

NEW REQUIREMENTS FOR C&E EXPERTISE ON BOARDS AND KEY BOARD AND EXECUTIVE COMMITTEES SHOULD BE CONSIDERED

One significant observation from the symposium was that compliance and corporate integrity efforts might be strengthened through targeted reforms that focus on governance and boards. In particular, it was suggested that, to the extent that board oversight is key to supervising the compliance function and setting "tone at the top," having more C&E expertise represented directly in the membership of boards could be a useful way to boost board effectiveness. One participant suggested that if the aim is to make C&E oversight a stronger or more explicit priority at the board level, one possible step could be to create new board-level committees that focus specifically on these issues. There was some discussion about whether responsibility for C&E might more naturally sit with one of the existing board committees, such as audit or governance, but it was also suggested that aligning C&E with a new committee of its own could be a more effective way to elevate the salience of these issues for the board. One countercurrent that was expressed was a paradoxical concern about funneling C&E matters to a board committee and the possibility that this might lead the full board to feel less responsible for playing a leadership role on ethics and tone at the top. It was suggested that this kind of responsibility was something that ought to be "owned" by the entire board, even if a specific board committee has a delegated responsibility for coordination with the CECO, receiving regular updates regarding the internal reporting function, and so on.

THE SEC SHOULD PUBLICIZE MORE REGULATORY DATA IN SUPPORT OF STRONG COMPLIANCE EFFORTS AND OFFER INCENTIVES TO CREATE A ROBUST CECO ROLE

Another theme in the conversation involved the importance of concrete regulatory data and positive SEC feedback as factors that could empower internal reporting and compliance mechanisms more generally. One participant observed that a basic challenge for CECOs in pushing stronger reporting channels and compliance efforts has been the inability to make the case that the investment pays off in the form of demonstrable reductions in risk and liability. A second participant said that it would be helpful to compliance officers to have SEC data on the numbers of companies and people under investigation, prosecutions, and settlements connected with internal and external whistleblowing tips, as well as data on firms that receive credit or lenient treatment from the SEC for strong internal compliance or reporting processes: "This is information that could be taken back to the board to show the benefits you get by reducing the likelihood of an insider going to the SEC with a whistleblower claim." According to another participant, although government agencies broadly disclose information on enforcement, the message that "compliance counts" in SEC enforcement decisions resulting from whistleblower tips is currently thin on the ground. It was suggested that this kind of information from the SEC, which would show that the agency cares about and responds to compliance efforts within firms, could have a significant impact on what companies do as a result. As one participant noted, "It makes a big difference to be able to say, 'In this case, the regulator specifically recognized the compliance efforts and mechanisms of the company as a mitigating factor in enforcement.' We can take examples like that and then use them to nudge companies, to get them to upgrade their programs and shift their cultures." Still another participant pointed out that judicial and law-enforcement authorities do consider the successfulness of internal reporting in detecting fraud in various prosecution and sentencing decisions, adding that the regulatory community needs to wrestle further with how to disclose this information to the corporate community in a useful way.

A related discussion at the symposium involved the notion that stronger standards and protections concerning the CECO role could be built into the enforcement side of the Dodd-Frank whistleblower rules. It was observed that, in much the same way that the CECO role has been defined via the Federal Sentencing Guidelines and then used as a factor in sentencing leniency, so too might the SEC consider similar factors as a basis for leniency in fraud and whistleblower cases. One participant asserted that empowering compliance and internal reporting mechanisms requires a strong CECO figure within management, and, absent that, the SEC should regard a company as effectively without a compliance program for the purposes of Dodd-Frank. In turn, that kind of SEC recognition and policy could serve as an important driver for more robust compliance efforts within firms. In a similar vein, another symposium participant emphasized that the CECO is particularly responsible for helping employees come forward via internal reporting and that formal SEC and U.S. Department of Justice endorsement of that responsibility could help better define the CECO role for corporate boards and management. With regard to compliance and ethical culture, one participant noted more broadly, "Where everyone is responsible for feeding the dog, the dog dies." By extension, empowerment and recognition of the CECO role by the SEC could be an important element of the agency's Dodd-Frank enforcement posture, particularly in aligning the new whistleblower rules with stronger internal compliance efforts.

TANGIBLE STEPS CAN BE TAKEN TO REINFORCE C&E AND INTERNAL REPORTING LINES, SUCH AS ADDRESSING EMPLOYEE FEARS ABOUT RETALIATION AND INEFFECTIVE FOLLOW-THROUGH

Another major strand of discussion in this symposium session touched more deeply on the practical steps needed to make C&E and internal reporting channels work more effectively and to encourage employees to use internal reporting in disclosing allegations of fraud and misconduct. One participant commented that "most employees want to do the right thing for the right reason," and, by extension, the main challenge for internal corporate reporting is to give employees a visibly safe pathway for doing so. Another echoed this observation: "Most employees are dedicated, loyal, and willing to go internally within the system, but you have to protect them in order for them to do that." A third said, "Employees need to be told and convinced that they are protected and that there is merit to coming forward. So, what incentives can be put in place [to help that to happen]?" A fourth observed that the ultimate success of internal reporting—and of the Dodd-Frank whistleblower regime in general—will be measured in particular corporations by "people feeling that the culture will fully support someone who wants to stand up and raise their hand to report a problem. But this will involve [building better] culture, as well as closing all of the [institutional] loopholes to prevent retaliation."

It was broadly observed during the symposium that there are two basic problems that often contribute to employee distrust in internal reporting processes. One is the possibility of retaliation (and perceived lack of management commitment to preventing it), and the other is the perception that management will not intervene or follow through effectively on the tips received through the internal reporting channel. If the ultimate aim is to make internal reporting more attractive to employees, then both of these concerns need to be addressed. Discussion at the symposium touched on several different, tangible steps that could be taken to pursue this end—all dedicated to better implementation, follow-up, and training surrounding the internal reporting mechanism and hotline.

One basic suggestion for strengthening internal reporting processes involved simply affirming the confidentiality of the reporting hotline and making that confidentiality very clear to all employees in a company. It was also noted that most of the inquiries that actually get reported to internal hotlines actually pertain to human-resource problems or other employment issues not related to fraud. Even so, the way in which a company handles these inquiries sends an important signal to employees about the seriousness and trustworthiness of the internal reporting channel. A related comment was that a basic challenge for internal hotlines and reporting involves "how you communicate to the caller that responsive action has been taken." That participant continued, "Demonstrating the effectiveness of reporting in little matters is a way to establish internal credibility for the effectiveness of reporting so that when bigger problems arise later on, the [hotline or reporting mechanism] is viewed as a viable option." A third participant suggested that a generic way to provide feedback to employees on internal reporting involves giving general-level information that the company has taken appropriate action and publicizing disciplinary cases and their outcomes after removing identifying details from those cases. "This tends to be a good strategy [for reinforcing reporting lines], because these cases [of effective discipline] then become the stories that people tell around the water-cooler," the participant said.

Other complementary suggestions for strengthening trust in internal reporting included more training for employees, stronger and more effective processes for internal investigation, and incentives for better management support for the reporting hotline and related investigations and processes. All these suggestions involve ways to bolster the credibility of reporting and investigation processes within corporations and to suggest that anti-corruption and anti-retaliation efforts are taken seriously by management. In principle, such steps can also help contribute to an "ethical culture" within a firm by conveying the same values to employees and affirming that there is a safe internal pathway that can be followed when misconduct or other problems arise.

INTERNAL REPORTING AND EXTERNAL WHISTLEBLOWING NEED NOT BE VIEWED AS ANTITHETICAL AND MUTUALLY EXCLUSIVE

One observation made during the symposium was that the availability of the external whistleblowing channel does not necessarily need to undermine internal reporting, even though Dodd-Frank makes the former available without requiring that employees first run the gauntlet of the latter. Although concerns were expressed about some of the specific contours of Dodd-Frank—and about the wisdom of whistleblower incentive payments more generally—several participants suggested that there might be significant common ground between the two approaches, and even that the Dodd-Frank whistleblower pathway might be leveraged to help reinforce or affirm internal reporting practices. One participant asserted that Dodd-Frank sets a stage by establishing strong rewards and protection for anti-fraud disclosures by employees and that a positive corporate response could involve getting out in front of Dodd-Frank, explaining that anti-fraud is a major priority for the company and that the internal controls and reporting mechanisms are intended as a primary device to that end. That person continued, "If the employee can get [an SEC] bounty anyway, why should the corporation sit back passively and just let the SEC dole these out?" By jumping in and acknowledging the SEC pathway, the company has the opportunity to reinforce its own credibility and to encourage the use of its own internal reporting channel for the vast majority of instances of misconduct (most of which, presumably, will not rise to the level of material damages that would make a Dodd-Frank bounty available).

Another symposium participant suggested that "Dodd-Frank is something that the corporate community should look on as an opportunity, rather than a negative." Although it was noted that SEC payments would indeed be available to whistleblowers in some instances, it was also pointed out that there is considerable nuance in how the law is likely to affect the litigation of fraud and misconduct in practice. For minor episodes of workplace misconduct or fraud, it seems unlikely that any insider would qualify for a Dodd-Frank whistleblower award, much less that regulators would be willing to devote time and resources to pursuing such cases. And for major episodes of fraud, the corporation already has an obligation to come forward and disclose those incidents to the SEC, and it faces the likelihood of significant fines or penalties regardless of whether a whistleblower is involved in reporting the violations. The most difficult cases are likely to involve a middle ground, in which instances of fraud might be material and a company might ideally want to detect and respond to those problems as quickly as possible through its own compliance mechanisms. What, exactly, is the right balance of regulatory authority and corporate interest in these situations remained a subject of open debate.

A third symposium participant offered a useful comment about resolving this situation, however. According to this participant, one of the chief aims of the compliance function in any organization is to convince employees that "they are responsible for ethics and compliance" by "making it personal all the way down the chain from the CEO through middle management." The idea is to convey to each employee that "your job is to report [instances of fraud or abuse], because the livelihood of the company and of your own position depends on it." If this kind of mentality and culture become pervasive in an organization, the internal reporting mechanism is likely to be far more effective as a result. By extension, it follows that the underlying occurrence of fraud—and of employees seeking to circumvent internal reporting in favor of direct access to the SEC—would likely be reduced as well.

ONGOING DIALOGUE BETWEEN THE COMPLIANCE COMMUNITY AND THE SEC CAN HELP FACILITATE MORE EFFECTIVE INTERNAL AND EXTERNAL REPORTING PROCESSES AND BETTER COMPLIANCE EFFORTS IN THE FUTURE

The concluding theme of the discussion in this session of the symposium touched on the potential for an ongoing conversation between the corporate compliance community and the SEC, which could help empower the former while refining the balance of the Dodd-Frank whistleblower policy and enforcement. One participant observed that the compliance community would surely benefit from ongoing SEC input on what the profession can do better and what the agency's immediate concerns and enforcement priorities are with regard to whistleblower issues. It was also suggested that regular contact between the SEC and members of the compliance community might be helpful to the agency as well. In this regard, many around the symposium table agreed that, whatever the potential putative merits or drawbacks of the Dodd-Frank whistleblower rules, the primary intent of Congress and federal policymakers was not to sabotage internal compliance efforts in corporations. Rather, the intent was to improve on efforts to combat fraud while recognizing that one of the most important resources for detecting such fraud is insider tips. It was also suggested that the compliance community can offer a unique window on the performance and challenges of internal compliance efforts and on the potential impact of the new whistleblower rules on those efforts.

Several participants offered the observation that nobody's interest is well served by undermining compliance and internal reporting within companies. In principle, everybody's interest is served through better early detection efforts and through better prevention, focusing on fraud and misconduct. It was again suggested that the ideal world would be one in which internal compliance and reporting are strong, the occurrence of corporate misconduct and fraud is low, and the use of the SEC whistleblower pipeline by insiders is correspondingly infrequent. Given this vision for the future, the question then becomes how companies and the SEC can broadly work together to move in this direction. It was suggested that ongoing dialogue between the SEC and the compliance community could offer a useful channel for feedback on the impact of Dodd-Frank by encouraging information-sharing on the incidence and outcomes of actual whistleblower claims and the challenges companies face in more effectively policing themselves.

APPENDIX A: SYMPOSIUM PARTICIPANTS

Michael D. Greenberg (Symposium Chair)
Director, RAND Center for Corporate Ethics and Governance

Donna C. Boehme (Symposium Co-Chair)
Principal, Compliance Strategists LLC

Urmi Ashar
President, National Association of Corporate Directors, Three Rivers Chapter; Trustee, Excela Health

Stephen Cohen
Deputy Chief, Enforcement Division, U.S. Securities and Exchange Commission

Keith T. Darcy
Executive Director, Ethics and Compliance Officer Association

Randy DeFrehn
Executive Director, National Coordinating Committee for Multiemployer Plans

James N. Dertouzos
Director, RAND Institute for Civil Justice

Paula J. Desio
Former Deputy General Counsel, U.S. Sentencing Commission

Charles M. Elson
Edgar S. Woolard, Jr., Chair and Director, Weinberg Center for Corporate Governance, University of Delaware

Patrick J. Gnazzo
Senior Vice President and General Manager for the U.S. Public Sector, CA Technologies (retired)

John P. (Jack) Hansen
Executive Fellow, Center for Business Ethics, Bentley University; Immediate Past Chair, Compliance and Ethics Committee, Association of Corporate Counsel

Chuck Howard
Partner, Shipman and Goodwin

Peter E. Jaffe
Chief Ethics and Compliance Officer, AES Corporation

Fred Kipperman
Senior Director of Strategic Relationships, RAND Corporation

Stephen Kohn
Executive Director, National Whistleblowers Center

Alexandra Reed Lajoux
Chief Knowledge Officer, National Association of Corporate Directors

Sean McKessy
Head of Whistleblower Office, U.S. Securities and Exchange Commission

Joseph Murphy
Director of Public Policy, Society for Corporate Compliance and Ethics; Of Counsel, Compliance Systems Legal Group (retired)

Steven Pearlman
Partner, Seyfarth Shaw LLP

James Thomson
President and Chief Executive Officer, RAND Corporation

Harold J. Tinkler
Chief Ethics and Compliance Officer, Deloitte LLP and the Deloitte U.S. Firms (retired)

APPENDIX B: SYMPOSIUM AGENDA

For Whom the Whistle Blows:
Advancing Corporate Integrity and Compliance Efforts in the Era of Dodd-Frank

Sponsored by

ethics·point *integrity at work*   SEYFARTH SHAW LLP *ATTORNEYS*

May 11, 2011
RAND Corporation Pentagon City Offices
Symposium Chair: Michael D. Greenberg
Symposium Co-Chair: Donna C. Boehme

Agenda

1:00 p.m. Welcome and Introductory Remarks
James Thomson, President and Chief Executive Officer, RAND Corporation
Michael D. Greenberg, Director, RAND Center for Corporate Ethics and Governance

1:10 p.m. Invited Remarks from Four Panelists
Introductions by Donna C. Boehme, Principal, Compliance Strategists LLC
* New Whistleblower Policies and Incentives: A Paradigm Shift from "Oversight" to "Insight"
  Steven J. Pearlman, Partner, Seyfarth Shaw LLP

* The Impact of *Qui Tam* Whistleblower Rewards on Internal Compliance
  Stephen M. Kohn, Executive Director, National Whistleblowers Center

* An Insider's Perspective on Whistleblowing Programs
  Patrick J. Gnazzo, Senior Vice President and General Manager for the U.S. Public Sector, CA Technologies (retired), and Joseph Murphy, Public Policy Chair, Society of Corporate Compliance and Ethics and Of Counsel, Compliance Systems Legal Group (retired)

2:00 p.m. Roundtable Session 1: Exploring the New World Order: Whistleblower Challenges for Corporate Management and Governance
Introduction by Harold Tinkler, Chief Ethics and Compliance Officer, Deloitte LLP and the Deloitte U.S. Firms (retired)

3:15 p.m. Break

3:25 p.m. Roundtable Session 2: Corporate Integrity in the Wake of Dodd-Frank: How Do We Fortify Internal Compliance, Reporting, and Culture?
Introduction by Keith Darcy, Executive Director, Ethics and Compliance Officer Association

4:40 p.m. Closing Remarks
Michael D. Greenberg

APPENDIX C: INVITED PAPERS FROM PANEL PARTICIPANTS

NEW WHISTLEBLOWER POLICIES AND INCENTIVES: A PARADIGM SHIFT FROM "*OVERSIGHT*" TO "*INSIGHT*"

Steven J. Pearlman, Partner, Seyfarth Shaw LLP[1]

Amended Remarks, Originally Presented on May 11, 2011

INTRODUCTION

In the wake of the bankruptcy of Enron in 2001, Congress developed a keen desire to understand the antecedents of corporate scandal and to identify ways to prevent similar catastrophes in the future. Policymakers became particularly interested in employee whistleblowing, given the context of executive whistleblower Sherron Watkins'[2] warning of Enron's likely demise.[3] Some in Congress asked probing questions about the potential for insider whistleblowing and the role that it might have played in preventing or mitigating the Enron meltdown. Could the disaster have been averted if Ms. Watkins spoke up sooner? Why didn't she speak up sooner? And why did others at Enron not blow the whistle?

Congress reacted to perceived disincentives to corporate insider whistleblowing by enacting Section 806 of the Corporate and Criminal Fraud Accountability Act of 2002 (Sarbanes-Oxley, or SOX).[4] The aim of that statutory provision was to protect whistleblowers against retaliation, with the hopes that conscientious corporate insiders like Ms. Watkins would come forward earlier and with less fear of retribution. Section 806 reflected only a small part of the SOX legislation, which more broadly involved a set of requirements for companies to develop compliance mechanisms, such as anonymous compliance procedures, independent audit committees, codes of ethics and conduct, and internal financial controls. Taken together, SOX's whistleblower protection provision and internal compliance requirements reflect a system

---

[1] Steven J. Pearlman is a partner in Seyfarth Shaw LLP's Labor and Employment Department and co-chair of the firm's Sarbanes-Oxley Whistleblower Team. Erin McPhail Wetty, an associate at Seyfarth Shaw LLP, assisted in researching the issues in this white paper.

[2] Notably, before Enron's collapse, another whistleblower informed the Internal Review Service (IRS) that Enron was using improper tax shelters to generate fictitious income. David S. Hilzenrath, "IRS Pays Enron Whistleblower $1.1 Million," *Washington Post*, March 15, 2011, http://www.washingtonpost.com/business/economy/irs-pays-enron-whistleblower-11-million/2011/03/15/ABFLAEb_story.html. Over a decade later, the IRS paid the whistleblower (who has remained anonymous to the public) a $1.1 million reward—the maximum award permitted under federal law at the time of the complaint. *Id.*

[3] "Enron Whistleblower Tells of 'Crooked Company,'" Associated Press, March 15, 2006, http://www.msnbc.msn.com/id/11839694.

[4] 18 U.S.C. § 1514A(a), The Corporate and Criminal Fraud Accountability Act of 2002, Pub. L. 107-204, 116 Stat. 745, enacted July 30, 2002.

designed to encourage corporate self-policing while treating the whistleblower as a key asset to that end.

Over the last few years, the plaintiffs' bar and whistleblower advocacy groups raised concerns that too many SOX whistleblowers' claims were being dismissed on what they characterized as technicalities.[5] Those concerns became a focal point for congressional action as policymakers considered a new round of corporate governance and regulatory reforms in the wake of the financial crisis of 2008. The existing whistleblower incentive structure changed dramatically on July 21, 2010, when Section 922 of the Dodd-Frank Wall Street Reform and Consumer Protection Act was enacted.[6] Section 922 offers employees a bounty for insider reporting of original information regarding fraud to the U.S. Securities and Exchange Commission (SEC), where that information leads to recovery exceeding $1 million. Available bounties under the statute may sometimes be enormous, as they may range from 10 percent to 30 percent of the SEC's total recovery. There is no statutory penalty to whistleblowers for failing to report alleged abuses in a timely manner or for failing to report them internally. Thus, Dodd-Frank manifests a paradigm shift away government "*over*sight" to government "*in*sight," as Section 922 arguably deputizes company employees as government agents and bounty hunters.

Modifications in the federal whistleblower regime under Dodd-Frank raise troubling policy questions about exactly what the government is trying to achieve and whether the new law will yield perverse consequences. There is notably a fundamental difference between this new incentive structure and the original policy behind SOX. Under the SOX whistleblower regime, employees who uncovered fraud were incentivized to report it internally immediately, so that the company could conduct prompt investigations and take appropriate remedial steps. That incentive structure was theoretically aligned with the company's and shareholders' interests. Now, however, employees who discover potential fraud may have incentives to defer reporting and let instances of fraud "mature" (the bigger the economic damage, the higher the bounty) and then to bypass internal compliance mechanisms by going straight to the SEC (in order to claim a bounty). To the extent that this kind of logic dominates employee behavior in practice, it is likely to frustrate the internal reporting policy behind SOX and to undermine shareholders' interests. In the corporate community, related concerns have been raised that the Dodd-Frank incentives may also encourage employees to submit meretricious and opportunistic complaints.

These kinds of arguments about Dodd-Frank invite basic concerns about what the response of employees to the new law will be, whether whistleblower bounty provisions can be reconciled with the aim of fostering robust corporate compliance mechanisms, and whether the ultimate effect Section 922 will be to undermine internal compliance efforts while degrading trust and ethical culture in the workplace. These concerns are sufficiently serious to merit

---

[5] "Whistleblowers Are Left Dangling," *Wall Street Journal*, September 4, 2008.
[6] 15 U.S.C. §§ 78u-6, 78u-7; Section 922 of Dodd-Frank is codified as Section 21F of the Securities Exchange Act of 1934.

careful scrutiny, even apart from the prospect that Dodd-Frank will prompt a rush of new whistleblower claimants to the SEC.

THE LEGAL LANDSCAPE

SOX Section 806

Anti-Retaliation: The Burden-Shifting Framework of Section 806 and Common Defenses

Employee claims under Section 806 of SOX have proliferated in recent years. Section 806 prohibits employers from retaliating against employees who complain about a purported violation of "section 1341 [mail fraud], 1343 [wire fraud], 1344 [bank fraud], or 1348 [securities fraud], any rule or regulation of the Securities and Exchange Commission, or any provision of Federal law relating to fraud against shareholders."[7] A plaintiff pursuing a Section 806 claim must establish a *prima facie* case with a "preponderance of the evidence" establishing that (1) she or he engaged in protected activity, (2) the employer knew or suspected that the employee engaged in a "protected activity," (3) she or he suffered an unfavorable personnel action, and (4) the protected activity *contributed* (it need not be the dominant factor) to the unfavorable personnel action.[8] If a plaintiff meets this burden, the employer then must establish by "clear and convincing evidence" that it would have taken the same action vis-à-vis the plaintiff in absence of the protected activity.[9] This burden-shifting framework is slanted intentionally in favor of the whistleblower and is in stark contrast to the framework in employment discrimination statutes like Title VII of the Civil Rights Act of 1964.[10]

Courts have imposed a number of important limitations on Section 806 claims. For example: (1) a complaint must "definitively and specifically" relate to the types of fraud enumerated in Section 806;[11] (2) the employee must have a subjectively and objectively reasonable belief that the complained-of conduct amounts to fraud;[12] (3) the fraud must be clearly articulated to the individual who allegedly engaged in retaliation;[13] (4) the alleged fraud must be on shareholders (courts are split on this issue);[14] and (5) the fraud must be material to investors.[15]

An illustration of the limitations courts have imposed on Section 806 claims, particularly the requirement that a whistleblower must have an objectively reasonable belief that the company engaged in the types of fraud exhaustively enumerated in Section 806, is the District

---

[7] 18 U.S.C. § 1514A(a).

[8] *Id.* § 1514A(b)(2)(C); 29 C.F.R. § 1980.104(b)(1).

[9] 18 U.S.C. § 1514A(b)(2)(C); 29 C.F.R. § 1980.109.

[10] *McDonnell Douglas Corp. v. Green*, 411 U.S. 792 (1973).

[11] See *Day v. Staples, Inc.*, 555 F.3d 42, 54 (1st Cir. 2009).

[12] See *Gale v. U.S. DOL*, Case No. 08-CV-14232, 2010 U.S. App. LEXIS 13104, *9 (11th Cir. June 25, 2010).

[13] See *Platone v. U.S. DOL*, 548 F.3d 322, 327 (4th Cir. 2008).

[14] Compare *Bishop v. PCS Admin. (USA) Inc.*, Case No. 05-CV-5683, 2006 U.S. Dist. LEXIS 37230, at *30-*31 (N.D. Ill. May 23, 2006) with *Reyna v. Cibagra Foods, Inc.*, 506 F. Supp. 2d 1363, 1381-83 (M.D. Ga. 2007).

[15] See *Fredrickson v. The Home Depot USA, Inc.*, Case No. 07-100, 2010 DOLSOX LEXIS 47, at *13-*14 (ARB May 27, 2010).

of Maryland's decision in *Harkness v. C-Bass Diamond, LLC*.[16] Ms. Harkness, a general counsel, claimed that she was retaliated against in violation of Section 806 for complaining that the company's president improperly disclosed to an outside investor that the company would be restating its earnings.

The company moved for summary judgment, arguing that Ms. Harkness lacked a reasonable belief that it violated securities laws because it was privately traded at the time of the disclosure and the plaintiff failed to adequately investigate whether the securities law regulation prohibiting such conduct (Regulation FD) applied, given that the company had not yet become publicly traded. Granting the company's motion, the court held that Ms. Harkness lacked a reasonable belief because she failed to research whether Regulation FD applied (or to direct outside counsel or others she supervised to do so). The court highlighted her lengthy professional experience in stressing that she should have researched or directed others to research the law for her claim to be legally cognizable.

In essence, then, SOX Section 806 is an employer anti-retaliation statute. It seeks to encourage whistleblowers to come forward by providing an explicit framework for redress in the event of retaliatory behavior by management. It also implicitly creates an incentive for firms not to retaliate against whistleblowers because of the threat of subsequent employment litigation in the event they do so.

The Interdependency Between SOX Section 806 and the Sections of SOX Requiring Companies to Institute Compliance Mechanisms

Section 806 was crafted to work hand-in-glove with other sections of SOX to attempt to provide shareholders maximum protection. More specifically, other sections of SOX require employers to establish robust internal compliance mechanisms, such as anonymous reporting procedures (§ 301),[17] independent audit committees (*id.*), effective internal financial controls (§ 404),[18] and comprehensive codes of ethics and conduct (§ 406).[19] In part, the policy behind this framework was to incentivize employees to report fraud internally so that companies could draw on their internal compliance machinery to promptly investigate the fraud in a manner calculated to protect investors. More broadly, this combination of provisions under SOX was also intended to compel firms to develop a robust set of internal compliance mechanisms and controls, in the belief that internal policing and controls are a key resource for preventing and remediating instances of corporate misbehavior and corruption. Consistent with the policies and aims of SOX, companies have devoted tremendous resources to developing internal compliance programs and mechanisms, consonant with the requirements of SOX.

---

[16] Case No. 08-CV-231, 2010 U.S. Dist. LEXIS 24380 (D. Md. Mar. 16, 2010).
[17] 15 U.S.C. § 78j-1.
[18] *Id.* § 7262.
[19] *Id.* § 7264.

Prominent *Qui Tam* and Related Whistleblower Protection Laws

Federal *Qui Tam* Laws

In contrast to Section 806 of SOX, several other federal statutes contain "*qui tam*" provisions that forcefully encourage whistleblowing. Simply stated, *qui tam* statutes establish penalties for unlawful conduct and allow whistleblowers to obtain a cut of the government's recovery. The most prominent *qui tam* statute is the federal False Claims Act (FCA), which empowers individuals to file a lawsuit on behalf of the government alleging fraudulent activities by government contractors or companies that receive or use government funds.[20]

Pursuant to the FCA, a whistleblower (called a "relator") may receive a bounty of between 15 percent and 25 percent of the amount recovered by the government.[21] Many believe that the FCA "has been the most successful avenue to date for whistleblowers."[22] Judgments and settlements procured under the FCA have exceeded $25 billion.[23] The top five awards are as follows: $1 billion (Pfizer), $900 million (Tenet Healthcare), $731.4 million (HCA), $650 million (Merck), and $631 million (HCA).[24] In fact, the government collected $3 billion in civil settlements and judgments under the FCA in 2010 alone.[25]

Similarly, there is an IRS whistleblower law that permits up to treble damages against companies responsible for tax fraud and offers whistleblower awards of between 15 percent and 30 percent of the amount recovered by the government.[26] In one prominent and recent example, a whistleblower received $4.5 million from the IRS for notifying the government about his employer's tax lapse (this award represents 22 percent of the taxes recovered).[27]

State Whistleblower Protections

Every state other than Alabama provides some form of whistleblower protection.[28] Twenty-five states have enacted their own false claim statutes. Moreover, 46 states have enacted statutory or common-law courses of action for whistleblower claims that provide for punitive damages.[29]

---

[20] 31 U.S.C. §§ 3729-3733.
[21] *Id.* § 3730(d)(1).
[22] Dori Meinert, "Whistle-Blowers: Threat or Asset?" *HR Magazine*, Vol. 56, No. 4, April 1, 2011.
[23] TAF Education Fund, False Claims Act Legal Center, "Top 20 Cases," undated, http://www.taf.org/top20.htm.
[24] *Id.*
[25] *Id.*
[26] 26 U.S.C. § 7623.
[27] "IRS Awards $4.5M to Whistleblower," Associated Press, April 8, 2011, http://www.fresnobee.com/2011/04/08/v-print/2341784/apnewsbreak-irs-awards-45m-to.html. See also note 2 *supra* regarding a recent $1.1 million award from the IRS to an Enron whistleblower.
[28] Meinert, 2011; *supra* note 22.
[29] *Id.*

To maximize the specter of sizeable damages, it has become common for plaintiffs to pursue whistleblower claims in federal court under federal whistleblower statutes and to tack on parallel state common-law or statutory claims.[30]

DODD-FRANK'S BOUNTY PROVISIONS

Despite this broad spectrum of powerful laws, the plaintiffs' bar and advocacy groups maintained that more extreme measures were needed to encourage employees to disclose fraud without fear of retaliation. Congress agreed and, on July 21, 2010, enacted Dodd-Frank,[31] which contains bounty provisions similar to the *qui tam* provisions in the FCA. Specifically, Section 922 of Dodd-Frank provides that a whistleblower may be eligible for a bounty of between 10 percent and 30 percent of the SEC's recovery where she or he voluntarily provides original information to the SEC that leads to the successful enforcement of a federal court or administrative action in which the SEC obtains monetary sanctions totaling over $1 million.[32]

On May 25, 2011, the SEC released rules to implement Dodd-Frank's bounty provisions.[33] Like the statute itself, the rules do not require employees to complain internally before blowing the whistle to the SEC.[34] Rather, the SEC proposes to use its discretion in setting bounty amounts to encourage whistleblowers to use internal compliance procedures before contacting the SEC.[35] This case-by-case discretionary approach amounts to having a policy to have no policy on orderly or timely complaints.

Further, the proposed rules offer whistleblowers who complain internally before complaining to the SEC a 120-day grace period so that the whistleblower keeps her or his "place in line." Put differently, if the employee complains to the SEC within 120 days after complaining internally, then the SEC will consider the date the employee complained internally as the date of original disclosure for purposes of determining whether the employee is eligible for a bounty. The rules also provide that, where a whistleblower reports original information through a company's internal compliance channels and the company then reports the

---

[30] Steven J. Pearlman, "Modern SOX Whistleblower Litigation in Illinois," *Law360*, February 8, 2010.

[31] Codified at 15 U.S.C. §§ 78u-6, 78u-7.

[32] 17 C.F.R. § 240.21F-3(a). Dodd-Frank also contains anti-retaliation provisions that protect whistleblowers (regardless of whether they qualify for a bounty). 17 C.F.R. §§ 240.21F-2(b), 240.21F-16(a). In addition, it is worth noting that, before Dodd-Frank was enacted, the SEC maintained a rule against insider trading that included a *qui tam* provision, SEA § 21A(e), previously codified at 15 U.S.C. § 78u-1(e). It allowed informants to receive up to 10 percent of amounts recovered by the SEC. *Id.* This provision was limited to insider trading violations, and, as a result, there were few and relatively minimal awards under it. Dodd-Frank repealed this rule. Dodd-Frank § 923(b)(2)(B).

[33] As of this writing, the final rules had not yet been published in the *Federal Register* but may be accessed at http://www.sec.gov/rules/final/2011/34-64545.pdf.

[34] See also the SEC's Proposed Rules for Implementing the Whistleblower Provisions of Section 21 F of the SEA, Exchange Act Release No. 63,237, November 3, 2010, at 35 n. 40, 51.

[35] *Id.*

information to the SEC, all of the information the company provided to the SEC will be attributed to the whistleblower. In other words, under such a scenario, the whistleblower will be credited for any additional information the company's investigation generated.

In addition, the following types of information will not qualify as being derived from the type of "independent knowledge" that forms the basis for a cash bounty under Section 922: (1) information determined to be subject to the attorney-client privilege; (2) information obtained as a result of legal representation; (3) information obtained through an engagement required under securities laws by an independent public accountant if the information relates to a violation by the engagement client or the client's directors, officers, or other employees; (4) information obtained by officers, directors, trustees, or partners of an entity who are informed of allegations of misconduct or who learn the information in connection with the entity's processes for identifying, reporting, and addressing possible violations of the law (such as a helpline); (5) information obtained by employees whose principal duties involve compliance or internal audit responsibilities or employees of outside firms retained to perform compliance or internal audit work; (6) information obtained in a manner that is determined by a domestic court to violate applicable federal or state criminal law; or (7) information that is obtained from a person who is subject to the above exclusions, unless the information is not excluded from that person's use or the whistleblower is providing information about possible violations involving that person. Of course, the whistleblower is given immunity for infractions of company policy.

There are broad exceptions to the foregoing limitations. For example, in certain circumstances, compliance and internal audit personnel, as well as public accountants, could become whistleblowers when the whistleblower believes her or his disclosure may prevent substantial injury to investors.

THE COSTS ATTENDANT TO THIS PARADIGM SHIFT

Incentivizing "citizen crime-fighters" may make good sense in certain contexts. For example, in this post-9/11 world, some find it comforting when they hear announcements at airports that everyone should keep their eyes and ears open for suspicious conduct and promptly report it to security personnel. Many also sleep better at night knowing that law-enforcement agencies offer financial rewards to individuals who provide tips that help solve crimes. But the whistleblower provisions under Dodd-Frank involve a very different sort of vigilante reporting and introduce new possibilities for conflict of interest and moral hazard in the workplace. The key question we need to ask about Section 922 follows: What is the downside of injecting a citizen crime-fighter, "bounty-hunter" mentality into the workforce?

I would argue that the Dodd-Frank whistleblower incentive structure undermines the balance established by SOX and is actually contrary to shareholders' interests. This is so for the following reasons:

- Dodd-Frank Section 922 has the potential to eviscerate the internal compliance mechanisms that companies have expended significant resources developing. As a result, companies may be deprived of an opportunity to conduct prompt and thorough investigations, and to take remedial measures, when instances of fraud do occur. This is a result that is likely to be bad for public policy and bad for investors and corporate bottom lines as well.

- Section 922 creates an incentive for employees with information about fraud or misconduct to allow problems to grow without internally reporting them, so that the SEC's eventual recovery, and the whistleblower's corresponding bounty, will be higher. This is in stark contrast to SOX, which established whistleblower protections in concert with requirements for internal compliance, controls, and methods to investigate potential fraud.

- Section 922 is very likely to engender distrust between management and employees. In particular, an opportunistic employee may be guided by a profit motive to search for information that could cast the company in an unfavorable light to the SEC. This kind of motive will compromise employee relations and have a chilling effect on broader information-sharing within organizations—another result with potentially far-reaching negative consequences.

- Finally, Section 922 also raises the specter that a blizzard of frivolous or undeveloped tips could lead to unwarranted and disruptive government scrutiny.

Without diminishing the value and laudable purpose of whistleblower laws or the importance of cases where good-faith whistleblowers have achieved sizeable recoveries, the substantial incidents of unfounded whistleblower complaints that were pervasive well before bounties under Dodd-Frank were available cannot and should not be overlooked.[36] The frequency of non-meritorious whistleblower complaints will almost certainly increase in the future, given the prospect of potentially enormous new bounties.

---

[36] Fraud statistics compiled by the Civil Division of the U.S. Department of Justice for 1987–2010 indicate that the government intervened as a claimant in fewer than 25 percent of *qui tam* lawsuits brought. Moreover, in the vast majority of *qui tam* cases where the government did not intervene, those cases were dismissed without payment. See fraud statistics and information on *qui tam* intervention decisions and case status released by the U.S. Department of Justice, Civil Division, in "Fraud Statistics—Overview, October 1, 1987–September 30, 2010," November 23, 2010, http://www.fcaalert.com/uploads/file/Stats%281%29.pdf.

THE IMPACT OF *QUI TAM* WHISTLEBLOWER REWARDS ON INTERNAL COMPLIANCE

Stephen Martin Kohn, Executive Director, National Whistleblowers Center

Amended Remarks, Originally Presented on May 11, 2011

On July 21, 2010, the Dodd-Frank Wall Street Reform and Consumer Protection Act was signed into law. This statute created new whistleblower protections and amended the Sarbanes-Oxley Act (SOX). Two provisions of Dodd-Frank require the U.S. Securities and Exchange Commission (SEC) and the U.S. Commodity Futures Trading Commission to pay monetary rewards to whistleblowers who provide original information regarding fraud to the commissions. Under these provisions, whistleblowers are entitled to a reward of between 10 and 30 percent of the total sanction obtained by the commissions.

The public interest is served by creating policies that encourage the reporting of suspected violations to the appropriate authorities, regardless of whether those authorities are a first-line supervisor, a corporate hotline, or a government official.

This paper carefully analyzes the reporting behaviors of employees, with a focus on what steps corporations or the government must take in order to ensure that fraud is reported in a timely manner and that markets are free from distortions caused by corruption. The paper focuses on the impact of whistleblower-reward programs for fraud detection and whether these laws will have a long-term negative impact on internal compliance programs.

Summary of Findings

- In cases under the False Claims Act, the overwhelming majority of employees utilize internal reporting procedures despite the potential for obtaining large external rewards: Empirical data show that approximately 90 percent of employees who filed a *qui tam* case initially reported their concerns internally, either to supervisors or to compliance departments.
- The existence of whistleblower rewards had no negative impact on the performance of compliance personnel: Only 4 percent of employees who filed a *qui tam* case worked in compliance departments.
- Whistleblower reward programs are highly effective in assisting in the detection of fraud and the enforcement of anti-corruption laws.
- Whistleblower reward programs should be expanded, and corporations should initiate internal reward programs.

Part I: Employee Reporting Behavior

Consistent with the findings of other organizations that have scientifically studied fraud-detection mechanisms, the 2010 Global Fraud Study published by the Association of Certified Fraud Examiners (ACFE) concluded that employees/"tipsters" are the most important source of information on fraud. The ACFE made the following finding: "While tips have consistently been the most common way to detect fraud, the impact of tips is, if anything, understated by the fact that so many organizations fail to implement fraud reporting systems." More specifically, the ACFE study analyzed a sample of more than 1,800 incidents of corporate and organizational fraud reported by examiners between 2008 and 2010. Insider tips accounted for the detection of fraud in more than 40 percent of the cases studied. Moreover, according to the ACFE's data, tips were as important as the next three most common methods of detecting fraud *combined*.[1]

In a complementary vein, the Ethics Resource Center (ERC) studied employee reporting behavior trends between 2000 and 2009.[2] Like the report issued by the ACFE, the ERC's study was based on scientific surveying methods as applied in the National Business Ethics Survey during those years.

According to the ERC's survey findings, approximately 40 percent of employees who witness fraud or misconduct do not report it to *anyone*. The percentage of employees who failed to report fraud during 2000–2009 remained relatively constant, even after the enactment of SOX. Moreover, the overwhelming majority of employees who did report fraud or misconduct did *not* utilize "hotlines" and never reported their concerns to proper law-enforcement authorities. Rather, about 75 percent of employees who reported fraud did so either to their own supervisors or to higher management.

The ERC concluded that the failure of employees to report misconduct was a *major problem* impacting the effectiveness of both internal corporate compliance programs and government law enforcement: "One of the critical challenges facing both E&O [enforcement and compliance] officers and government enforcement officials is convincing employees to step forward when misconduct occurs."

Part II: The False Claims Act Data Demonstrates the Success of *Qui Tam* Laws/Rewards Programs in Ensuring Corporate Compliance

The False Claims Act (FCA), originally enacted in 1863, is the preeminent whistleblower reward law. In its modern form, it has been in existence since 1986. Other state and federal whistleblower reward programs were modeled on this act, including the reward provisions in the Dodd-Frank Act. The law prohibits fraud in government contracting and procurement and

---

[1] See Association of Certified Fraud Examiners, *Report to the Nations on Occupational Fraud and Abuse*, Austin, Tex., 2010, http://www.acfe.com/rttn/rttn-2010.pdf.

[2] See Ethics Resource Center, *Blowing the Whistle on Workplace Misconduct*, Arlington, Va., December 2010, http://www.ethics.org/resource/blowing-whistle-workplace-misconduct.

contains a whistleblower reward provision that entitles whistleblowers to qualify for a reward ranging from 15 percent to 30 percent of the monies recovered by the United States from corrupt contractors.

Objective statistics published every year by the U.S. Department of Justice Civil Fraud Division[3] unquestionably demonstrate the success of the FCA. Whistleblowers have successfully exposed billions of dollars in fraud in the last two decades, and they are, by far, the single most important source of credible information documenting illegal contracting/procurement practices.

Since the enactment of the FCA, the amount of overall civil recoveries obtained annually by the United States has dramatically increased, from $89 million in 1986 (prior to the whistleblower reward program) to $3.08 billion in 2010. Furthermore, it is now well documented that whistleblower disclosures are responsible for the *majority* of all federal fraud recoveries from dishonest contractors.

The act's statistics actually undervalue the contribution of whistleblowers because they do not quantify the deterrent effect achieved when the law is enforced. When a company is able to pay the penalties mandated under law, the United States usually requires these companies to enter into extensive compliance agreements that help prevent future fraud. Thus, the deterrent value of the law is not currently subject to objective quantification.

When the Department of Justice statistics are viewed in relation to the findings of the ERC and ACFE, the reason for the success of the FCA is evident. The act combines the fact that employee whistleblowers are the single most effective force in detecting real-world fraud with a direct financial incentive to uncover and disclose fraudulent conduct.

The importance of using financial incentives to promote corporate fraud disclosures was also underscored in a published scholarly study by the University of Chicago's Booth School of Economics, which affirmed that a *qui tam* reward program is indeed the best way to pursue workplace misconduct.[4]

Part III: Impact of *Qui Tam* Laws on Internal Reporting

The existence of a *qui tam* whistleblower reward program should have no significant impact on the willingness of employees to internally report potential violations of law or to work with their employer to resolve compliance issues. This point is underscored by a recent National Whistleblowers Center (NWC) study in which a systematic sample of more than 150 *qui tam* cases filed under the FCA during 2007–2010 was retrieved and analyzed. Findings from

---

[3] See U.S. Department of Justice, Civil Division, "Fraud Statistics—Overview, October 1, 1986–September 30, 2008," http://www.justice.gov/opa/pr/2008/November/fraud-statistics1986-2008.htm. See also U.S. Department of Justice, Civil Division, "Fraud Statistics—Overview, October 1, 1987–September 30, 2010," November 23, 2010, http://www.crowell.com/pdf/FalseClaimStat.pdf.

[4] See Alexander Dyck, Adair Morse, and Luigi Zingales, *Who Blows the Whistle on Corporate Fraud*, Chicago, Ill.: University of Chicago, September 2009, http://faculty.chicagobooth.edu/luigi.zingales/research/papers/whistle.pdf.

the study demonstrated that approximately 90 percent of all employees who would eventually file a *qui tam* lawsuit initially attempted to resolve their disputes internally.[5]

These empirical findings are consistent with those reported by other recent studies. For example, in its May 13, 2010, issue, the *New England Journal of Medicine* published a "Special Report" examining the behaviors of *qui tam* whistleblowers who won large FCA judgments against the pharmaceutical industry.

That study found that "nearly all" of the whistleblowers "first tried to fix matters internally by talking to their superiors, filing an internal complaint or both." More specifically, the study found that more than 80 percent of interviewed *qui tam* claimants had attempted to report instances of fraud internally within their companies prior to filing claims under the FCA.[6] The journal's conclusion that "nearly all" of the whistleblowers tried to report their concerns internally is entirely consistent with the larger study conducted by the NWC and stands squarely contrary to the concerns raised by industry that "greedy" employees will avoid internal compliance programs in pursuit of "pie-in-the-sky" rewards. The truth is that the overwhelming majority of employees who eventually file *qui tam* cases first raise their concerns within the internal corporate process.

Part IV: Impact of *Qui Tam* Laws on Compliance Reporting

The NWC study also found that the existence of large *qui tam* rewards did not cause compliance employees to abandon their obligations and secretly file FCA cases to enrich themselves:

- Approximately 4 percent of plaintiff employees who filed *qui tam* cases under the FCA worked in compliance departments.
- Only one plaintiff employee contacted a government agency without first raising the concern within the corporation.

Of those compliance-relators, only *one case* concerned an employee who reported his concerns directly to the government without first trying to resolve the issue internally. That case, *Kuhn v. Laporte County Comprehensive Mental Health Council,* was clearly an exception. In *Kuhn,* the U.S. Department of Health and Human Services Inspector General was conducting an audit of the company's Medicaid billing. During the audit, the whistleblower learned that the company's internal "audit team" was altering documents to cover up "numerous

---

[5] See National Whistleblowers Center, *National Whistleblowers Center Report to the Securities and Exchange Commission*, Washington, D.C., December 17, 2010, http://www.whistleblowers.org/index.php?option=com_content&task=view&id=1169.

[6] See Aaron S. Kesselheim, David M. Studdert, and Michelle M. Mello, "Whistle-Blowers' Experiences in Fraud Litigation Against Pharmaceutical Companies," *New England Journal of Medicine*, Vol. 362, No. 19, May 13, 2010, pp. 1832–1839.

discrepancies," including "forged" signatures and so-called "corrections" to "billing codes." The employee reported this misconduct directly to the U.S. Attorney's Office. The disclosures to the government were *not* provided as part of a *qui tam* lawsuit. Instead, the employee believed that these disclosures would help "protect" the employer from "federal prosecution" based on the voluntary disclosures.

Indeed, this case highlights exactly why it is important to permit compliance employees to report directly to the government. When the compliance department itself is engaged in misconduct, where else could this whistleblower have gone?

Part V: Reports to Internal Compliance Must Be Fully Protected

In a December 15, 2010, letter to the SEC, the Association of Corporate Counsel stated that corporate attorneys "value . . . effective corporate internal compliance and reptting systems." The association went further and argued that "in-house counsels are the pioneers in establishing and facilitating corporate whistle-blowing systems and safeguards."[7] The evidence simply does not support this claim. First, there is no support in the record that current "corporate culture" encourages and rewards employees who blow the whistle. That is why Congress enacted § 21F of the Securities and Exchange Act—precisely to help create such a new culture. Second, corporate counsel has, for years, argued in court that employee contact with internal programs was *not* a legally protected whistleblower activity. The detrimental impact of these arguments on employee perceptions of internal compliance programs is obvious and has likely contributed to the phenomenon of "hollow" or "check-the-box" compliance programs in at least some organizations.[8]

In the area of whistleblowing, in-house counsels have actively and aggressively undermined internal compliance programs for over 25 years. Since as early as 1984, corporations and their attorneys have consistently argued that employees who report to internal compliance programs are *not* whistleblowers and are *not* protected under whistleblower laws. One of the first such cases was *Brown & Root v. Donovan*, in which a quality assurance inspector was fired after making an *internal* complaint about a violation of law.[9]

In that case, President Ronald Reagan's appointed Secretary of Labor ruled that such internal disclosures were in fact protected and ordered the whistleblower to be reinstated.

---

[7] See Association of Corporate Counsel, "Proposed Rules for Implementing the Whistleblower Provisions of Section 21F of the Securities Exchange Act of 1934, File No. S7-33-10," letter to Elizabeth Murphy, U.S. Securities and Exchange Commission, December 15, 2010, especially p. 3, http://www.acc.com/aboutacc/newsroom/loader.cfm?csModule=security/getfile&pageid=1233871.

[8] See Donna C. Boehme, "From Enron to Madoff: Why Many Corporate Compliance and Ethics Programs Are Positioned for Failure," in Michael D. Greenberg, *Perspectives of Chief Ethics and Compliance Officers on the Detection and Prevention of Corporate Misdeeds: What the Policy Community Needs to Know,* Santa Monica, Calif.: RAND Corporation, CF-258-RC, 2009, pp. 27–32, http://www.rand.org/pubs/conf_proceedings/CF258.html.

[9] The case is available at http://www.whistleblowers.org/storage/whistleblowers/documents/DoddFrank/brown&rootv.donovan.pdf.

Brown & Root disagreed and appealed the case to the U.S. Court of Appeals for the Fifth Circuit. That court agreed with Brown & Root and upheld the termination. The employee's career was ruined because he failed to raise his concerns to government officials. The Fifth Circuit explicitly held that, to be a whistleblower, an employee must contact a "competent organ of government."

Since that date, in court after court, corporate attorneys have aggressively argued that internal reports are not protected. There is not one reported case in which a company argued that employees who disclosed allegations to compliance departments should be protected as a matter of law. Indeed, even the under the FCA, employers have consistently shot themselves in the foot by arguing that employees must provide their information to government authorities in order to receive statutory protection from retaliation.

Below are examples of judicial holdings under the FCA in which the court supported the company and took positions that undermined internal compliance programs:

> "'An employee's investigation of nothing more than his employer's non-compliance with federal or state regulations' is **not enough to support a whistleblower claim.**" *Hoyte v. American Nat'l Red Cross*, 518 F.3d 61 (D.C. Cir. 2008)

> "The record quite clearly shows Hopper **was merely attempting to get the School District to comply with Federal and State regulations. Her numerous written complaints, seventy letters and over fifty telephone calls were all directed toward this end . . . she was not whistleblowing.**" *US ex rel. Hopper v. Anton*, 91 F.3d 1261 (9th Cir. 1996)

> "It is true that Brandon used terms like 'illegal,' 'improper,' and 'fraudulent' when he confronted the shareholders about the billing practices. . . . **Brandon was simply trying to convince the shareholders to comply with Medicare billing regulations. Such conduct is usually not protected.**" *Brandon v. Anesthesia & Pain Management*, 227 F.3d 936 (7th Cir. 2002)

> "Simply reporting [a] concern of mischarging . . . does not establish that [plaintiff] was acting in furtherance of a qui tam action. . . . **He did not communicate that he was going to report the activity to government officials.**" *Hutchins v. Wilentz*, 253 F.3d 176 (3rd Cir. 2001)

Part VI: The Sarbanes-Oxley Act Prohibits Rules That Could Interfere with Whistleblower Disclosures

The regulated community cannot lawfully create any rule that would create a financial disincentive or otherwise discourage a person from filing a complaint with the SEC or disclosing potential criminal conduct to law enforcement.

SOX creates near-absolute protection for employees who contact any federal law-enforcement agency regarding the violation of any federal law. Section 1107 of SOX *criminalizes* any attempt to interfere with the right of any person to contact the SEC concerning any violation of law. Section 1107 reads as follows:

"Whoever knowingly, with the intent to retaliate, takes any action harmful to any person, including interference with the lawful employment or livelihood of any person, for providing to a law enforcement officer any truthful information relating to the commission or possible commission of any Federal offense shall be fined under this title or imprisoned not more then 10 years, or both." Codified at 18 U.S.C. § 1513(e)

Congress reaffirmed the policies behind Section 1107 when it enacted the Dodd-Frank Act. The definition of a protected disclosure under Dodd-Frank explicitly includes disclosure directly to law enforcement as covered under section 1107 of SOX.

Part VII: Whistleblower Reward Laws Should Be Implemented
The historical success of the FCA demonstrates the effectiveness of whistleblower reward programs. Based on that success, and on the objectively demonstrable track record of *qui tam* enforcement under the FCA, Congress has expanded the scope of these programs. Given the critical role employees play in fraud detection, it is safe to assume that the new *qui tam* laws now embedded in the internal revenue code, the Securities Exchange Act, and the Commodity Exchange Act will likewise prove successful and fuel the expansion of new whistleblower reward programs.

The private sector should not respond to these developments by trying to reverse a progressive trend. Instead, corporations should acknowledge the ameliorative impact of these programs and seek to build upon them by implementing internal incentives to encourage internal fraud reporting by employees. When implementing such internal reward programs, corporations should ensure the following: (1) the entitlement to the reward must be guaranteed by contract and enforceable in court, (2) the size of the rewards must be competitive with the rewards of the federal government, (3) the right to counsel must be guaranteed, (4) strict anti-retaliation protections must be adhered to, and (5) the company must consent that filing such a reward would constitute a protected act under SOX and applicable state laws.

AMENDMENT TO STEPHEN KOHN'S REMARKS, JUNE 2011:
THE IMPACT OF THE SEC'S FINAL RULES ON INTERNAL COMPLIANCE

Among the most controversial provisions of the Dodd-Frank Act is its mandate that employees who report major fraud to the U.S. Securities and Exchange Commission (SEC) can obtain financial rewards. In passing the act, Congress invited public debate over these reward provisions. Congress required the SEC to undergo a formal public rulemaking proceeding before it implemented final regulations controlling the reward provisions. The SEC was required to solicit and review public comments and justify its final rule in light of those comments.

The whistleblower rulemaking proceeding sparked vigorous public debate. The most contentious issue concerned the role of internal corporate compliance. On the one hand, the corporate community, led by the U.S. Chamber of Commerce, expressed concern that employees would bypass existing compliance programs in order to file claims directly with the SEC and obtain monetary rewards. The chamber and its allies supported a rule that would have required employees to raise concerns to their internal compliance programs before they could seek a reward from the SEC.

On the other hand, whistleblower advocacy groups, including the National Whistleblowers Center (NWC), strongly supported protecting employees who raised their concerns directly with the SEC. They pointed out that public policy encourages all citizens to report potential criminal activities to law enforcement at the earliest possible time and that the federal Obstruction of Justice Statute prohibits all restrictions on the right of employees to report potential crimes to law-enforcement officials.

Recognizing that each side in this debate raised valid concerns, the NWC proposed a compromise position. The NWC urged the SEC to define whistleblower disclosures to include reports to internal corporate compliance programs. In other words, regardless of whether the employee reported his or her concern to the SEC or to an internal compliance program, the employee would obtain equal protection and equal eligibility for a reward.

In its December 17, 2010, rulemaking proposal, the NWC set forth its position as follows:

> Given the Commission's stated commitment to fostering effective internal compliance programs . . . the Commission should establish a rule that contacts with internal compliance departments and employee supervisors have the same protection as contacts with the SEC.
>
> All contacts with an Audit Committee or any other compliance program shall be considered, as a matter of law, an initial contact with the SEC . . . . Should an internal complaint result in a finding of a violation, and lead to the Commission issuing a fine, penalty or disgorgement, the employee whose application was submitted through the internal complaint process shall be fully eligible for a reward.[10]

---

[10] See National Whistleblower Center, *Impact of Qui Tam Laws on Internal Corporation Compliance*, Washington, D.C., December 17, 2010, p. 12, http://www.whistleblowers.org/index.php?option=com_content&task=view&id=1169.

This proposal encourages employees to utilize compliance programs while at the same time encouraging corporations to empower compliance officials to ensure that their programs work. The rule would ensure that employees who chose to work within corporate structures had the same rights as those who reported directly to the SEC.

On May 25, 2011, the SEC issued its final rules. Commission Rule 21F-4(c)(3) adopted the NWC's compromise proposal. The SEC defined a whistleblower disclosure to include disclosures made "through an entity's internal whistleblower, legal, or compliance procedures."

Rule 21F-4(c)(3) should encourage corporations to create independent and effective compliance programs managed by empowered compliance officials. Given an option to report a concern to a truly independent compliance program or taking the extraordinary step of reporting a potential violation to the government, the overwhelming majority of employees would choose the internal program. The ball has been handed to the corporations themselves to demonstrate that their workplace cultures have changed, that whistleblowers are now welcome, and that compliance programs will be independent and empowered.

AN INSIDER PERSPECTIVE ON WHISTLEBLOWER PROGRAMS

Patrick Gnazzo, Senior Vice President and General Manager for the U.S. Public Sector, CA
Technologies (Retired)

Joseph Murphy, Director of Public Policy
Society of Corporate Compliance and Ethics; Of Counsel,
Compliance Systems Legal Group (Retired)

Remarks Presented on May 11, 2011

Introduction

Whistleblowers in any context are always controversial. Certainly in the corporate world, where competition in the marketplace drives the environment and leaks of confidential information can damage a company's competitive position, the thought of someone taking the company's business outside to others draws a strong negative reaction. Add to this the specter of extensive government investigations, possible prosecution and unwelcome press attention, and the prospect of a proposal that would enrich those who blow the whistle to the government, and the situation has predictably caused great concern in the corporate world. Yet in the current political environment, the reality is that encouragement of whistleblowers and increasing protection of those who raise issues appear to be a fact of life.

In this context, how should corporate managers deal most effectively with these circumstances? Current whistleblower laws, particularly those that offer a financial incentives to reporters, such as the False Claims Act and its new cousin, Dodd-Frank and its controversial bounty provisions, raise a key question for management: Are companies, through their compliance and ethics programs, properly positioned to withstand increased whistleblower challenges? And what can the SEC and companies do together to support both internal compliance and ethics programs and external whistleblower mechanisms? To these questions, the authors offer an "insider" perspective, speaking as former chief ethics and compliance officers (CECOs)—persons whose job commonly involves developing, implementing, and overseeing the internal employee reporting line, which, in turn, is a foundational element of a strong company compliance and ethics program and culture.

Role of the Internal Employee Reporting Program

Internal whistleblowers received a big boost with the adoption of the U.S. Organizational Sentencing Guidelines in 1991,[1] when the U.S. Sentencing Commission (USSC),

---

[1] Part 8 of the Federal Sentencing Guidelines, covering sentencing guidelines for organizations, is sometimes known as the "U.S. Organizational Sentencing Guidelines." See Paula Desio, *An Overview of the Organizational Guidelines*, Washington, D.C.: U.S. Sentencing Commission, undated, http://www.ussc.gov/Guidelines/Organizational_Guidelines/ORGOVERVIEW.pdf.

in reviewing organizational misconduct, developed several mitigating factors that could reduce an organization's fines. One of these was the existence of an effective program to prevent and detect crime. The USSC enumerated seven core elements that needed to be included in such a program. Among these standards was providing a means for employees to raise issues within the organization without fear of retribution. In order to create a means for employees to come forward safely, corporations typically instituted third-party helplines to protect the anonymity of the reporting employee. Again, an employee reporting line is commonly managed by the CECO of the corresponding organization. The CECO uses the information received through the line to initiate internal investigations, where appropriate. Allegations and the results of investigations are then reported by the CECO to management and to the board of directors. At least, that is the way it's *supposed* to work if there is an effective employee reporting line and a strong, independent CECO reporting to a properly committed management team and a compliance-savvy board of directors.

The USSC's model has become an increasingly common one globally, and the promotion of internal company reporting systems has become a key part of the effort to prevent corporate crime and unethical conduct. And over the last two decades, industry has responded by instituting programs that give voice to employee concerns.[2]

Controversy: Impact of the Dodd-Frank Whistleblower Provision on the Corporate Compliance and Ethics Program

From the company perspective, since the 1991 adoption of the U.S. Organizational Sentencing Guidelines (and before, in a few industries), corporations have gone to some length to develop compliance and ethics programs to prevent and detect crime and other misconduct. In particular, they have installed employee reporting lines for those who seek to raise concerns. Many have retained outside firms so the lines can be staffed around the clock and are able to handle calls in numerous languages. Some have added online, web-based reporting systems. Some have even established ombudsman systems, giving employees numerous options for reporting issues.[3] This has not been without substantial expense and some considerable pain for the compliance and ethics professionals who championed these systems.

Now many of these professionals and their managers see the potential for their work to be undermined.[4] They see the SEC offering potentially staggering financial rewards to those

---

[2] In 2002, Congress further underscored the role of the internal reporting line by enacting Section 806 of the Corporate and Criminal Fraud Accountability Act of 2002 (commonly known as "Sarbanes-Oxley"), 18 U.S.C. §1514A(a), enacted July 30, 2002.

[3] See Transparency International, "Interview with Michael Monts" (vice president for business practice at United Technologies), September 2008, and Charles Howard, *The Organizational Ombudsman: Origins, Roles and Operations—A Legal Guide*, Chicago, Ill.: American Bar Association, 2010.

[4] One of the strongest industry objections to the new Dodd-Frank whistleblower bounty provisions is that internal corporate compliance programs will be undermined. See Association of Corporate Counsel,

who turn in their employers. Some even see the threat of false complaints by employees as a means of revenge, or subtle extortion by employees faced with adverse employment action. They might even see their management questioning the wisdom of having a compliance program under these circumstances. After all, a cynic might argue, the more you teach the employees about the law, the more likely they are to think they see violations and run to the government to collect the bounty.

There has been a general fear expressed in commentary on the proposed Dodd-Frank whistleblower rules that employees will now call the government first, seeking personal enrichment. But studies on what drives whistleblowers commonly reveal another side to this issue. If an employee does not call internally, typically it is not because "they don't pay enough." Bounties are not new; years of experience under the False Claims Act, which can provide rich rewards to whistleblowers, still shows that employees usually raise their issues internally, even with no prospect of financial reward for doing so. And while fear of retaliation may certainly be a factor in why employees do not report internally,[5] it is not the number one driver. Why do employees not report concerns? Because they expect nothing will happen. If there is no confidence that the caller will be listened to, why should an employee place his or her career in jeopardy?[6]

The typical whistleblower who goes outside the company has a common story to tell about his or her experience internally: "I tried to tell them at the company, but no one listened. And then I was given a poor evaluation and shown the door."[7] This point really drives what companies need to do. Will offering "mini-bounties" to employees drive their behavior? There are many skeptics who doubt the wisdom of such approaches, and even those who consider this tactic are typically not prepared to offer anything like what Dodd-Frank or the False Claims Act would provide. Instead, companies need to step up their game when it comes to implementing internal whistleblowing systems and ensuring the empowerment and independence of their compliance and ethics programs. But this is more easily said than done, and despite best intentions, many companies still fall short in this crucial implementation stage. Speaking, ourselves, as compliance and ethics professionals with a long experience in the field, both as in-house officers and lawyers and as outside experts, we can tell you that the thought of employees becoming rich at the company's expense by going first to the government frightens

"ACC Files Comments re: Dodd Frank Whistleblower Regs Proposal," press release, December 17, 2010, http://www.acc.com/advocacy/news/dodd-frank.cfm.

[5] See the Ethics Resource Center's 2010 *Report on Whistleblowing and Workplace Bullying*, which found that 15 percent of employees who reported misconduct perceived that they had been retaliated against (http://www.ethics.org/whistleblower).

[6] See Ethics Resource Center, *2009 National Business Ethics Survey*, 2009, http://www.ethics.org/nbes/downloadnbes.html.

[7] See National Whistleblowers Center, *Impact of* Qui Tam *Laws on Internal Compliance Programs*, December 17, 2010, http://www.whistleblowers.org/storage/whistleblowers/documents/DoddFrank/nwcreporttosecfinal.pdf.

management for several reasons. Foremost among these is that if someone reports wrongdoing outside the internal system, then there is no opportunity within the system to investigate and correct the issue before it becomes a public event. Obviously, there are many reasons why an organization would prefer not to have its issues of misconduct, along with the company's business details, made public. While there are obvious issues of embarrassment and potential loss of protected commercial trade secrets, there are other reasons that are often overlooked in the discussion. When a whistleblower goes outside, the matter may stay secret (in False Claims Act cases, the complaint is even filed under a court seal) for extensive periods of time, even for a number of years, while the government reviews the complaint and decides whether it will initiate an action against the organization.

The problem this poses is that if company employees are engaged in misconduct and this does not come to light within the organization for several years, then there is very little that a CECO can do to help management and the board of directors correct misdeeds and remove wrongdoers from the system until that information comes to light. This delay in organizations becoming aware of a whistleblower complaint becomes even more problematic when the issue reported may also involve a safety problem that necessitates an immediate fix to prevent injury or loss of life. Consider the impact of the typical Justice Department delay if the O-Ring defect in the space shuttle *Challenger* disaster had first been the subject of a filed *qui tam* action. Not as compelling, but important all the same, are instances in which employees raise substantive process and policy issues along with wrongdoing concerns. If the employee has incorrect information about the wrongdoing and only reports that concern outside the organization, then the process and policy issues may never come to light and therefore never get corrected.

Observations from the Trenches: Pros and Cons of Internal Helplines

Unfortunately, those of us in this room who are or have been CECOs or worked on these programs internally know that internal employee reporting lines do not always work the way they are intended. There are several reasons why. As noted above, the most common, but often overlooked, reason employees do not use a helpline is that they believe nothing will happen. In addition, the employees may not trust that they will be protected if they come forward to report internally. And, of course, in hard financial times, employees may tend to put their heads down simply for fear of losing their jobs or impacting the corporation's ability to withstand weak economic conditions.

On the management side, meanwhile, managers may find it very difficult to deal with anonymous allegations, and they may spend more of their energy attempting to find out who brought the allegation forward than they do in having the allegation investigated and resolved.

At least one "ostensibly anonymous employee hotline" was actually found to have rung directly on the desk of the CEO's secretary.[8]

Unfortunately, many managers and even boards erroneously believe it is enough to simply turn on the employee reporting line and put up a poster. But the reality is that the overwhelming majority of the work that will determine success comes after a complaint is received. There are so many ways that this can be mishandled that it takes very careful attention to run an effective system. While the high-profile failure at Renault, in which senior executives were sacked as a result of anonymous accusations before a professional investigation was conducted and before the managers were given an opportunity to respond, may not be typical, it certainly underscores the perils associated with reporting systems that are not managed professionally.[9]

So for internal reporting systems to operate credibly and effectively, there is much work to be done around appropriate implementation, non-retaliation, and effective follow-up and investigation. A candid assessment to evaluate how well the internal reporting line has been implemented, and effectively embedded into the culture of the company, is a good first step. The more the company is able to integrate the elements of a meaningful program into its operational protocols, such as those for hiring, training, communicating, promoting, evaluating, rewarding and disciplining employees, the more likely that it has created a culture in which people believe they can speak up safely and that something will actually be done when they do.

One of the most critical steps a company can take to ensure that an internal reporting system will actually work as intended (to prevent and detect wrongdoing) is to appoint an empowered senior-level CECO with the mandate, experience, positioning, and resources to develop an effective program, oversee the helpline, prevent retaliation, and monitor progress.[10] In a real sense, the CECO is the only person in the organization standing in between the whistleblower and those who would retaliate against him or her. When the CECO is weak or poorly positioned, it should be no surprise that even a well-designed program can fall apart, be inadequately implemented, or lose the confidence of employees. The USSC recognized the key role of the CECO to the success of internal programs when it recently supported the positioning of a chief compliance officer with "direct reporting obligations" to the governing authority.[11]

---

[8] See "Remarks by David Becker at the Practising Law Institute's Ninth Annual Institute on Securities Regulation in Europe," January 25, 2011, http://cfodirect.pwc.com/CFODirectWeb/Controller.jpf?ContentCode=EDYR-8DQLH6&ContentType=Content.
[9] See Donna Boehme, "About That Confidential Employee Hotline: An Open Letter to Boards, CEOs and Other Interested Stakeholders," Compliance Week, May 5, 2009.
[10] See Michael D. Greenberg, *Perspectives of Chief Ethics and Compliance Officers on the Prevention and Detection of Corporate Misdeeds*, Santa Monica, Calif.: RAND Corporation, CF-258-RC, 2009, http://www.rand.org/pubs/conf_proceedings/CF258.html, and Boehme, "From Enron to Madoff: Why Many Corporate Compliance Programs Are Positioned for Failure," in Greenberg, 2009.
[11] Under the 2010 amendments to the Federal Sentencing Guidelines, a company may receive credit for an effective compliance program even if "high-level personnel" are involved if a number of conditions

Similarly, the 2010 Organisation for Economic Co-Operation and Development's (OECD's) *Good Practice Guidance on Internal Controls, Ethics, and Compliance* recommends that the "senior corporate officer" leading the company's ethics and compliance efforts have "adequate level of autonomy from management, resources and authority."[12] Finally, a growing number of high-profile corporate settlements with global enforcers reflect heightened scrutiny on the role of the CECO, with some prosecutors requiring ongoing assurance that the CECO will have adequate independence, positioning, and direct, unfiltered access or a reporting line to the governing authority and the resources to do the job.[13]

Both Government Whistleblowing and Internal Reporting Lines Have Drawbacks

In our view, public-sector whistleblower mechanisms cannot replace internal compliance and reporting systems. Whistleblower laws and enforcement mechanisms are subject to some fundamental limitations and weaknesses, among them:

1. They can take a very long time to resolve claims.
2. Government resources are limited, so small claims may lose out as low-priority.[14]
3. The employee's name typically becomes evident, and for the most part, his or her career is ended.
4. If the organization is not found guilty or does not settle, then the whistleblower receives nothing.

Finally, whistleblower actions can be cumbersome, lengthy, and difficult to pursue, and in some instances, the adjudicating body, like the U.S. Labor Department for claims of financial wrongdoing under Sarbanes-Oxley, may know little or nothing about corporate finance and therefore have a difficult time resolving claims, leaving the whistleblower very little in the way of protection or compensation.

This being said, there are also some limitations and downsides associated with internal employee reporting lines, as well:

1. Employees may not believe any action will be taken.

---

are satisfied, including that the CECO has "direct reporting obligations" to the governing authority. See amendments to the Federal Sentencing Guidelines at http://www.ussc.gov/guidelines/2010_guidelines/Manual_PDF/Chapter_8.pdf.

[12] OECD, *Good Practice Guidance on Internal Controls, Ethics, and Compliance*, 2010, http://www.oecd.org/dataoecd/5/51/44884389.pdf.

[13] Examples of this significant trend are Tenet, Pfizer, and Bayer, all of which agreed in settlement agreements that the CECO would not be, and would not be subordinate to, the general counsel or the chief financial officer. See also Recommendation 8 of the BAE Systems Woolf Committee Report, *Business Ethics, Global Companies and the Defence Industry*, May 2008, http://ir.baesystems.com/investors/woolf.

[14] Although a "small claim" to government may be an extremely important compliance matter to an individual company.

2. Employees may not trust the protection promised by the organization.
3. It is difficult to investigate an allegation that comes in anonymously, especially when not enough of the facts are brought forward by the anonymous employee.
4. The employee who remains anonymous never receives recognition or compensation for coming forward to protect the organization.

Finally, CECOs will usually tell you that most of the issues that come through the employee helpline or hotline are unrelated to wrongdoing and are either personal or management relations issues (e.g., "I would like a closer parking space" or "employee bathrooms need to be cleaned") or are human resource issues (e.g., "I did not receive my performance evaluation" or "my boss doesn't like me"). Those kinds of issues can deflate management's view of the hotline's importance. Meanwhile, to the extent that those non-wrongdoing issues are not resolved and dealt with, employees may perceive the hotline as ineffective and may be therefore be less likely to come forward via the reporting line when it is really necessary to protect the organization from illegal acts.

While it can sometimes seem to skeptics that internal reporting lines are mere nuisance mechanisms, there is an important, but usually unstated, benefit that such systems bring. The line itself may not literally be the source of important reports of problems. Employees may, in fact, call other internal sources, including the compliance and ethics staff, human resources, internal audit, the legal department, and higher-level managers with concerns about wrongdoing. Yet, even though they may not use the reporting line itself, the existence of the line and its related publicity send a crucial message to everyone in the corporate community. The employee line is, in an important sense, a permission slip to all employees to raise issues through any available means.[15] It may be that most employee line calls are human resource matters, but the message sent by the existence of this system can be the very thing that causes a worried employee to raise the serious issues directly to the compliance officer or a business unit lawyer.

The existence of a well-working internal reporting line through which employees feel encouraged to raise concerns without fear of retaliation sends a strong message to employees that management "walks the talk" and thereby supports the culture of "doing the right thing" that is so critical to driving desired behavior and judgments within an organization. This is a benefit that is rarely if ever included when the number of reporting line calls is tabulated, but it is an important fact of corporate life and an essential reason to protect the integrity of internal reporting systems. Speaking as former in-house compliance and ethics professionals, we can attest to the necessity of a good employee internal reporting program and the strength that it brings to an organization's efforts to act with integrity. If management knows that employees can come forward with candor and anonymously report illegal activity, then they are less likely

---

[15] Discussed in "Interview with Michael Monts," 2008.

to engage in those illegal acts. Particularly when it takes more than one individual to engage in fraud, a co-conspirator can never be sure whether any of the other individuals who are party to the act will find it in their conscience to come forward and report. Nor do they know how many others around them suspect what is going on.

Thus, just the bare fact that the employee reporting program exists, is promulgated, and is supported by the company's highest authority does much for preventing bad acts from occurring in the first place. And where an internal employee communication program and reporting line are well implemented, that program will bring forward issues of wrongdoing that can be investigated and corrected before they impact customers, shareholders, and the company—a result that is much to be preferred to allowing externally raised claims to linger under seal for years while being addressed through a cumbersome and sometimes inadequate government whistleblower program. Again, whistleblower laws and enforcement are unlikely to be a substitute for an effective internal compliance program and employee reporting hotline. It is the job of senior management, the board of directors, and the CECO to develop and support a strong, open communication program and reporting line for employees so that the latter can come forward when they are concerned about irregularities and improper conduct.

Making Governmental Whistleblower Systems More Effective

In our view, government whistleblower programs can have greater value if properly administered and designed for quick resolution, and if regulators are willing to work cooperatively with company compliance and ethics professionals. In this way, future legislation and future improvements to government whistleblower programs should seek advice and information from compliance and ethics professionals like CECOs, who manage those programs internally for their organizations. Individuals who have been managing internal reporting lines and employee communication programs are well situated to explain the pitfalls that can accompany whistleblower allegations and the future adverse impact they may have on the whistleblower. They can also advise on what actually works in motivating employees and how government programs can promote valuable preventive efforts in companies.

Unfortunately, "whistleblower" is not a well-respected term today, even though whistleblowers have done enormous good in bringing illegal activity to the forefront. Whistleblowers need to be assured that their concerns will be effectively addressed and that they will receive protection from retaliation. Most importantly, organizations need stronger incentives and encouragement to manage effective internal communication programs to prevent, detect, and stop improper activity *before* it can impact the value of an organization and the financial protection of its employees' jobs and retirement savings.

Conclusion: How Government and Companies Can Work Together to Prevent and Detect Corporate Wrongdoing and Support Both Internal and External Whistleblower Programs

While we acknowledge the controversy that the Dodd-Frank whistleblower bounty provisions have caused in many quarters, we also note that the SEC has attempted to create a balance in its proposed rule-making: an equilibrium between the company's interest in resolving problems internally through strong compliance programs and the public's interest in providing direct access to federal whistleblower incentives and protections when internal programs fail. We are hopeful that this balance will be achieved in the final rules. In the meantime, we conclude by offering some additional thoughts on ways in which the SEC and companies could work together to support the prevention and detection of wrongdoing, whether internally or under the Dodd-Frank whistleblower program:

1. Establish a protocol for SEC discretionary referral of Dodd-Frank whistleblower matters to companies/CECOs for initial investigation, including matters to be considered for investigation, criteria, standards, and processes for determining whether a particular company warrants this level of trust.

2. Make clear that companies that show diligence in their commitment to compliance and ethics will benefit from leniency in the SEC's enforcement decisions under Dodd-Frank.

3. Establish a readily applicable protocol for determining eligibility for lenient treatment, based on a compliance and ethics program linked to an empowered CECO, including standards for determining whether a company has an empowered CECO who meets the test.

4. Form an informal compliance and ethics working group, including experienced CECOs, facilitated by a credible nonprofit organization (e.g., the RAND Center for Corporate Ethics and Governance), to work on these matters on an ongoing basis.

5. Review other steps the SEC can take to encourage stronger compliance and ethics programs (e.g., specifically include such efforts in the SEC penalty policy, provide more detail on the role of compliance and ethics programs in enforcement decisions).

REFERENCES

Black's Law Dictionary, 6th ed., St. Paul, Minn., 1990.

Boehme, Donna C., "From Enron to Madoff: Why Many Corporate Compliance and Ethics Programs Are Positioned for Failure," in Michael D. Greenberg, *Perspectives of Chief Ethics and Compliance Officers on the Detection and Prevention of Corporate Misdeeds: What the Policy Community Should Know*, Santa Monica, Calif.: RAND Corporation, CF-258-RC, 2009, pp. 27–32. As of August 8, 2011:
http://www.rand.org/pubs/conf_proceedings/CF258.html

Clark, Doug, "Opening the Floodgates: The Dodd-Frank Whistleblower Provisions' Impact on Corporate America," *Boardmember.com*, October 2010. As of June 24, 2011:
http://www.boardmember.com/Opening-the-Floodgates-The-Dodd-Frank-Whistleblower-Provisions-Impact-on-Corporate-America.aspx

Daly, Ken, President and CEO of the National Association of Corporate Directors, testimony before the House Subcommittee on Capital Markets and Government Sponsored Enterprises at the hearing "Legislative Proposals to Address the Negative Consequences of the Dodd-Frank Whistleblower Provisions," May 11, 2011. As of June 24, 2011:
http://www.sec.gov/comments/s7-33-10/s73310-312.pdf

Ethics Resource Center, *Blowing the Whistle on Workplace Misconduct*, Arlington, Va., December 2010. As of June 24, 2011:
http://www.ethics.org/files/u5/WhistleblowerWP.pdf

Greenberg, Michael D., *Perspectives of Chief Ethics and Compliance Officers on the Detection and Prevention of Corporate Misdeeds: What the Policy Community Should Know*, Santa Monica, Calif.: RAND Corporation, CF-258-RC, 2009. As of August 8, 2011:
http://www.rand.org/pubs/conf_proceedings/CF258.html

———, *Directors as Guardians of Compliance and Ethics Within the Corporate Citadel: What the Policy Community Should Know*, Santa Monica, Calif.: RAND Corporation, CF-277-CCEG, 2010. As of August 8, 2011:
http://www.rand.org/pubs/conf_proceedings/CF277.html

Kesselheim, Aaron S., David M. Studdert, and Michelle M. Mello, "Whistle-Blowers' Experiences in Fraud Litigation Against Pharmaceutical Companies," *New England Journal of Medicine*, Vol. 362, No. 19, May 13, 2010, pp. 1832–1839.

OECD—*see* Organisation for Economic Co-Operation and Development.

Organisation for Economic Co-Operation and Development, *Good Practice Guidance on Internal Controls, Ethics, and Compliance*, February 18, 2010. As of July 18, 2011:
http://www.oecd.org/dataoecd/5/51/44884389.pdf

Public Law 111-203, Dodd-Frank Wall Street Reform and Consumer Protection Act, July 21, 2010.

U.S. Chamber of Commerce et al., "File Number S7-33-10, Proposed Rules for Implementing the Whistleblower Provisions of Section 21F of the Securities Exchange Act of 1934, Release No. 34-63237 (Nov. 3, 2010)," letter to Elizabeth Murphy, U.S. Securities and Exchange Commission, December 17, 2010. As of August 8, 2011: http://www.centerforcapitalmarkets.com/wp-content/uploads/2010/04/SEC-WB-Comment-Letter-12-17-10.pdf

U.S. Sentencing Commission, *Guidelines Manual*, November 2010. As of July 18, 2011: http://www.ussc.gov/Guidelines/2010_guidelines/index.cfm